D0886976

Black Vanguards and Black Gangsters

From Seeds of Discontent to a Declaration of War

Steven R. Cureton

UNIVERSITY PRESS OF AMERICA,® INC.
Lanham • Boulder • New York • Toronto • Plymouth, UK

Copyright © 2011 by
University Press of America,® Inc.
4501 Forbes Boulevard
Suite 200
Lanham, Maryland 20706
UPA Acquisitions Department (301) 459-3366

Estover Road
Plymouth PL6 7PY
United Kingdom

Library of Congress Control Number: 2011925275
ISBN: 978-0-7618-5522-4 (clothbound : alk. paper)
eISBN: 978-0-7618-5523-1

Debbye and Nia
No blessings have come higher than you both

For the Martyrs of Revolution

There remains a necessary need for a revolution to liberate and reclaim the youth residing in ganglands. Thank you for sacrificing your blood and providing the blueprint. Our every action should be designed to immunize our youth against nihilism.

Contents

Preface

By Virtue of Birth,
What Are the Odds of Becoming?

I was born, kept living, and became what? I am a 1970's child who would eventually become a ward of the court in 1982. My biological father left me with hate because his absence forced me to endure the humiliation of feeling like my entire existence was a mistake. My less than conventional mother taught me independence and distrust because she was my primary first lady that would betray the fidelity of functional parenting. What are the odds that I would turn out to be a criminal and not an educated black man? With these ingredients it's a wonder that I did not end up a statistic. Fast forward to 1997 and I am not a criminal but a professor. I survived a private hell to obtain a doctorate in sociology from Washington State University. Seven years of attempting to prove myself worthy of a doctorate from a white ivory tower social structure is enough to bleach any black man's soul. My mentors Charles Tittle and Jim Short disciplined me to be a balanced sociologist; however, they failed to alert me to the other obligation that I could either accept or reject. I guess they thought, I would figure it out or maybe they just did not know how to engage me in a dialogue about race or maybe they thought, well I don't quite know what they were thinking. I do know that there is so much pressure to measure up to a dual standard, one held by the ivory structure and the other held by seemingly every black person that is aware of my doctorate status. I was so naïve to think that all I had to do was research, publish, teach, and serve the university on an administrative level. My early research on race and crime only proved that I could produce enough quantitative work to get tenure. I thought I was doing so well, I thought getting tenure meant I had arrived but it only meant I could get tenure.

I came across E. Franklin Frazier's "The failure of the negro intellectual" and after reading this, I concluded that I was a failed black intellectual given I had done nothing to advance a detailed understanding of the black experience as a product of integration. All I had done was explain the racial arrest differentials in the criminal justice system. According to Frazier, the black intellectual had "failed to dig down into the experiences of the Negro and provide the soul of a people" (Frazier, 1962:64). I agree with Frazier, that black scholars have a responsibility to research race legacy, holding blackness as a social product of integration. I am a firm believer that the black scholar has a critical responsibility to effectively communicate the social reality of black people. Frazier (1962) contends that black social scientists should produce worthwhile testimonies of the black experience. He further offers that the impact of urbanity on blackness deserves special attention. Hence, the main objective of this book is to address the question of "whether black gangsterism is the mark of oppression and/or a sense of otherness despite concentrated integration?"

I was born in Brooklyn, New York on September 14, 1968. I am the son of a non-conventional mother and absent father who was a musician and a man who brutally beat my mother. What dominates my memory, were the many 70's parties my mother hosted. The music, the food, the women, the alcohol and the bowls of marijuana joints were common for these parties. My brothers, sisters and I had to eat that "sleepy spaghetti" (spaghetti with crushed sleeping pills mixed in the sauce). Yes, mother wanted us sleep and out of the way so the party could proceed uninterrupted by us. We were a mischievous crew as we often managed to secure alcohol and those tiny white cigarettes that gave us the "funnies." Essentially, we were kids between the ages of five and twelve who on any given Friday or Saturday night would be doped up with sleeping pills, tipsy on alcohol and/or being silly because we smoked too many tiny white cigarettes that turned out to be marijuana joints. What's more when my mother's company became bored, we became their source of entertainment. We were snatched out of our sleep and forced to dance in our pajamas. Sleepy eyed, irritated and still buzzing, we burst out with dances (e.g. the boat row, the electric boogie, the punching man, the five step, the hustle, and the bump) to the music of James Brown (the Godfather of soul), Marvin Gaye (Prince of Soul), Parliament and Funkadelic. The living room was filled with smoke and the aroma of too many people in one space. I don't know if any of the party people were important movement or revolutionary figures because I never really heard any revolutionary slogans or black power messages. I do remember how songs like Sam Cooke's "A Change is Gonna Come," Marvin Gaye's "What's Going On," Stevie Wonder's "Living for the City," and the O'Jays "For the Love of Money" seemed to galvanize the spirit of the people at the party. Perhaps these songs represented some sort of acknowledgement of the hard times that blacks were experiencing on a daily basis. Nevertheless, I am willing to bet that there was the possibility that I danced before grass roots revolutionaries, pimps, pushers, hustlers, and gangsters or ordinary black people just trying to survive. My family was dependent on the government for medical care and food, and we lived in places where people were similarly dependent on the government for a basic standard of living. My home life was dysfunctional as I was exposed to a lot; however, the most damaging experiences were the routine realities of domestic violence, police and social workers. Outside the confines of our apartment was violence over what seemed to be trivial matters. There was so much hustling drugs, gambling, running numbers, liquor shot spots, and scamming that most kids felt this was a normal way of life. Arguably, dependency on the government for basic health care, food, housing, and education, perhaps pacified residents in my community. The awesome power of institutional marginalization apparently erased the desire for organized protests, especially in places where I lived (Maryland and Southeast side of the District of Columbia).

I will admit from five to about eleven years old I cried about everything, so I was what you would call a cry baby. At one particular 70's parties, I was crying because my mother made me take a cold bath in a tub that she had painted black. I cried because the water was cold and the tub was black. I thought all tubs were supposed to be white. A young man grabbed me and asked what was I crying about and I only cried harder at the sight of his afro, sideburns and goat-tee.

I remember him saying that "no one gives a fuck about black men crying so that means no one cares if your little ass is crying, so go ahead and do what your momma told you." I am now 42 years old and my life's experiences validate what this young man said to me. What he said certainly seems socially relevant for urban resident young boys who have to negotiate their masculinity within the context of an aggressive subculture of gangsterism. The following passage seems fitting as well,

After banging our heads against the walls of oppression and with a trickle of blood on our foreheads, we cried for our manhood. We cried for our manhood in the late night hours after experiencing a day littered with frustration over what we are not allowed to do, and who we are not allowed to become. We cried for our manhood as we watched you march into our communities, and infect our women and children with the idea that this community is void of real men. We cried in defiance after watching you drag our fathers off to prison. We cried for our manhood because we were just kids when you came to take the men in our lives away. We cried for our manhood when you bashed our heads and spilled our blood, and offered us destructive vices to cope with the nefarious conditions of the ghetto. We cried for our manhood as we watched our own black people leave us to the horrors of the ghetto. We cried for our manhood when we realized that the black church ministered to the people on the mountain top and not to the people in the valley. We cried for our manhood when we realized that there was no answer at the altar, we kept waiting for a change to come and it never did. We cried for our manhood when you said, your suffering does not matter, so we ain't crying no more. (Cureton, 2009: 347-348)

It remains an amazing ideological and practical failure that mainstream America continues to invest in the assumption that the legal, civil, economic, social, educational, and cultural concessions afforded to African-Americans produced a middle class that serves as evidence that the American creed (equality of life, liberty, and the pursuit of happiness) is inclusive of all citizens. What about the black people in the ghetto? All of the contemporary, seemingly recurrent themes of ghetto living become newsworthy creating what Keegan refers to as reasonable fears about black people, "there are reasonable fears about the deteriorating quality of neighborhood life, the effects of poverty and drugs, the gang wars, extortion, brutality. But these grim facts are not facts about black people; they are facts about ghetto life, whether black or white" (Keegan, 1971:31). The contemporary ghetto is a homeland without security, a homeland where dreamers become innocent criminals for no other reason except for investing in ideological goals of functional citizenship without adequate opportunities. The ghetto is a place where generations of blacks have been asking politely, "excuse me but what about us" and now a newer more volatile and more hostile generation of youth are shouting "what the fuck about us!"

Tucker (1968) argues that America should engage in a progressive effort to overhaul the living conditions of the inner city with the goal of eliminating ghetto conditions. Let's examine what Tucker offered about the socially damning facts about the ghetto.

We have seen that the Negro's heritage in America at best has been one of willful neglect at the behest of his white brother. At worst, it has been conscious subjugation by a white community which has stripped him of his manhood, his pride and his incentive by throwing him into the pit of the city and daring, indeed taunting, him to survive amidst squalor, disease, unemployment, depravity. What little the black man has left when he enters the city's bowels, the ghetto kills off forever. Everything, that is, but vengeance. For the street-corner test books of the inner city teach the lessons of hatred well, even to the student who refuses to listen. The depravity, the ugliness, the powerlessness, all combine to make learning easy. Classes are short-men graduate early. For years, the ghetto's hatred turned in on itself. Blacks victimized blacks, acting out street-corner dramas in uncontrolled rage, convulsed by spasms of self-hatred and masochistic feelings, lashing out at innocent brothers for the sake of conquering someone-anyone-to prove one's existence somehow mattered. (Tucker, 1968:123)

The ghetto seemingly is a sub-culturally specific, life course altering, environment where residents face realities that are more reflective of alien black colonies in an American promise land. What kind of psychic re-adjustments are necessary to cope with these types of life course realities? I wonder if mainstream Americans have any conscious awareness about what it means to have to negotiate a functional existence while doing life as a black male in a deprived and depraved environment. We need only be brave enough to journey to the bad side of town (regardless of who you are you most likely know about the bad part of town enough not to be caught anywhere near it) observe the streets, smell the air, taste the flavor of the foods, drink the water, and tune into the sounds to arrive at the conclusion that the images are volatile, streets are dangerous, the air is vapor, the food tainted, the water distastefully gritty, and the sounds deafening. What are the odds of making it out of the ghetto and becoming thoroughly grounded in functional citizenship? Alternatively, what are the odds of fidelity to constant reminders that the ghetto will always be home? By virtue of birth as a black male the odds of becoming anything worthwhile is contingent upon class stratification, socioeconomic status, and the power of human spirit.

Acknowledgments

For the sisters in the struggle, without you, we automatically lose! For every tear, for every second, minute, hour, day, week, month, and year that you gave and continue to give, thank you. For the young brothers living fast and dying young, death is forever and we need you here.

Chapter One

Seeding, Watering and Harvesting

The ultimate goal of this book is to explore the historical and contemporary realities of black gangsterism in America using a black sociological perspective. Black sociology focuses on the function(s) of race in America. Black sociology is based on the premise that the African-American experience in a democratic, capitalistic free market, resource and material based system exposed generations of blacks to a legacy of circumstances from which blacks' entire existence has been more about recovery, reclamation, and adaptation. Specifically, blacks' life chances is thoroughly stitched in the social fabric of this country, which consists of political and racial subordination, blocked opportunity structures, resource strain, psychological rejection and intimidation, denial of rights, substandard quality of life, institutional mass incarceration, inter and intra-racial, discrimination, segregation, isolation, and victimization. All of which became seeds of discontent from which a rebellious harvest featuring a black empowerment movement (ranging in approaches from passive, non-violent resistance to retaliatory defiance) emerged. Seemingly, the limited black masses who were in positions to take advantage of economic, social, and educational opportunities were more inclined to pursue legal challenges and were more concerned with integration and assimilation, which was best achieved by demonstrating unconditional compassion, love, and forgiveness. However, those unskilled, under-educated, unemployed, and/ or socially challenged blacks destined to remain in the "excluded" category gravitated towards aggressive defiance, physical posturing, and inter/intra-racial retaliation because of the perceived necessity to survive and desire to express rage. Instead of civil obedience and peace in urban ghettos, deviant, criminal and violent peer group activity became the dominant way to express social discontent (Dyson, 2000; Marable, 1996; Oliver, 1989; Staples, 1975; Staples, 1973; Gesehwender, 1971).

1

The challenge for the African-American male in America has been a constant struggle to reconcile the seemingly dominant social dynamic that black masculinity is significantly less human than white masculinity. There was no sanctuary for black men, as his worth was constantly devalued and/or presented as an infectious germ to his women and children. What should be expected of any man faced with such a disrespectful presentation? There is no course except to be violently dissatisfied with the American agenda to debase black humanity; however, what behavioral manifestations are best suited for a war against one's humanity? The answer is of course a revolution of some kind, a direct attempt to transcend powerlessness but whether a revolution was passive, proactive or aggressively reactive, government agencies at federal, state, and local levels endorsed tactics to eliminate any reaction that seemed to pose the slightest threat coming from black men (Garrow, 1981). Hence, the contemporary black male condition in America is littered with martyrs, assimilationists, and permanent outsiders.

Contemporary black gangsterism is an indication that the Black Power Movement, protest and revolutionary groups won some battles relative to social validation and civil entitlements but lost the war that should have eliminated opportunity blockages for the marginalized, powerless black residents of the ghetto. According to Huey P. Newton (co-founder of the Black Panther Party for Self-Defense), black males residing in socially disorganized environments routinely operate out of confusion, fear, and doubt related to the negative events that dominate their lives. Moreover, Newton argues that lower class black males are socially aware enough to perceive oppression but unfortunately don't have the social sophistication, resources and legitimate opportunities to effectively counter the stagnating consequences of oppression. These black men are therefore faced with respect and social identification issues and feel personally responsible for their social realities. This is a departure from common thought that lower class black men blame mainstream society for their shortcomings. For Newton, black men are handicapped by social and structural isolation, marginalization, poverty, and dysfunctional family dynamics, which makes them vulnerable to failure and open to digesting suggestions of inferiority (Hilliard and Zimmerman, 2006; Hilliard and Weise, 2002). It is simply unnatural for black men to accept an inferior status without some sort of social rebuttal (Jackson, 1994; Cleaver, 1968). Therefore it's probable that these men will invest in any rebellious group, especially if that group provides opportunities for lifestyle improvements and respect. It does not matter how these groups are perceived in mainstream America because these marginalized black men are operating outside of mainstream. Hence, it should be no surprise when marginalized black men decide to obey whatever, normative expectation, and/or associate with whatever group that seems to offer personal validation.

AMERICAN HYPOCRISY

The United States of America is comprised of institutions that promote freedom, equality, advancements opportunities, justice, and domestic tranquility. America was supposed to be a place where diverse groups of people through due diligence and hard work could be successful. The American ethic promoted the fact that investing in this country would be returned with acceptance and appreciation for patriotism. However, blacks' legacy in this country speaks to a reality that is altogether different, as they have dealt with governmental inconsistencies related to equitable citizenship entitlements. As a result blacks have had to contend with; "how they feel about this country and alternatively how this country feels about them?" Historically, black men have demonstrated ultimate patriotism by becoming soldiers for a country that would prefer they remain in servitude. Their willingness to support the United States during wartime (Revolutionary War, World Wars I and II, Korean, and Vietnam Wars) afforded the opportunity to dispel racial stereotypes by performing admirably during battle. However, the black soldier's courage, bravery, and death was not enough to change racial intolerance as this country (for the most part) maintained hatred for the human cargo it had imported from Africa (Magida, 1996; Anderson 1993; Bennett, 1983; Haley, 1964).

America has engaged in psychological warfare against black people (which seemed entrenched in religious ideology). During the 1800's and early 1900's, a significant number of white Americans remained faithful to the pure white righteousness and deservedness doctrine, which promoted elite/subordinate inter-racial human dominion and black exploitation for economic gain and societal progression. This white privilege doctrine dictated that blacks were not deserving of human equality because they were the offspring of sinister deities and therefore had souls that were not redeemable or worthy of salvation (Levin, 2002; Ezekiel 1995). Slavery and lynching were two social control mechanisms that mainstream religion in America failed to effectively directly confront. Slavery was wholesale debasement of blacks' humanity forget about the argument that it was human domestication for purposes of a better democracy and progressive capitalism. Slavery was a holocaust for Africans who became black in America.

Slavery was cultural thievery and spiritual annihilation and in the wake of this gross miscarriage of humanity, what was the African in America supposed to do? It is far too simplistic to say that Africa was stripped of approximately 40 million people who would face the horror of slavery in parts of the world that were both visible and invisible to the global community. Think of it this way, if 40 million African-Americans were lost to the slave trade, that would be equivalent to erasing the lives of every African-American (assuming blacks are actually 40 million of the 305 million) in the United States in 2010. The United States received slaves from the major slave ports of Africa for approximately 243 years (1619 to 1862). If we allow 30 years to remain the standard representation of a generation then the United States accepted human cargo for purposes of capitalism for a little over eight generations. Whatever economic, social, political, community, village and/ or tribal order; and whatever cultural ascriptions concerning the humanity of African blood; and whatever free spirit consciousness native to African soil would be forever compromised in unimaginable ways (Raboteau, 1978). The slaves' journey often began with dehumanization whether it came from African Kings, African appointed slave merchandisers or transporters, and/or European village raiders. Slaves endured physical duress, walking some 100 miles and thrown in small canoes, that would transport them to larger vessels (in cases where there were no immediate ports). The sources of slaves hailed from large kingdoms and small tribes of West Africa, and/or south of the Sahara, more specifically slaves hailed from the southern Atlantic coast (Angola and the Congo), Indian ocean's coast (Mozambique, Zanzibar) and the island of Madagascar, southern regions of the western Sudan, and areas nearing rivers (Senegal, Gambia, Volta, Niger and Congo). Still more slaves came from British (Accra, Cape Coast, Sherbro, Freetown, Komenda, Dixcove), French (Assinie), Dutch (Whydah, Elmina and Axim), Portugese (Luanda and Benguela), and Danish (Christianborg) controlled ports (West African coast). The Grain, Ivory and Gold coasts were represented by Bight of Benin, Ibo, Brass, Bonny, and Calabar slave ports, which more than likely siphoned human cargo from Sierra Leone, Liberia, Congo Angola, Bight of Biafra, Gambia, Nigeria, Senegal (Raboteau, 1978; Meier and Rudwick, 1966; Bennett, 1961). From these ports Africans endured the infamous Middle Passage (African coast to West Indies or American shores), which took two to three months and sometimes longer.

Africans were faced with conditions befitting of cargo, yet their humanity made them painfully aware of the overcrowding and cramped spaces and exposed them to hazardous air, disease, heat, hunger, brutality, violence, and whatever else European crews had in mind (torture, rape, and cold blooded murder). Without the experience of having been there, words cheapen the reality of the infamous passage; however, pause and consider the passage;

> She was the mother of all pearls, beautiful by design, rich in culture and was home to a spirited people, until she was raped. Africa suffered a volatile intrusion of its

interior body at the hands of Europeans and the result was the birth of slavery. The New World became 22 million African's final destination where a hostile race legacy would commence. Offering numbers only provide empirical estimations that can be reduced or added to depending on historical recordings; however, slavery was more than numbers the slave trade was not a statistic, however astronomical. The slave trade was people living, lying, stealing, murdering, dying. The slave trade was a black man who stepped out of his house for a breath of fresh air and ended up, ten months later, in Georgia with bruises on his back and a brand on his chest. The slave trade was a black mother suffocating her newborn baby because she didn't want him to grow up a slave (Bennett, 1982:29).

The Emancipation Proclamation was signed in 1863 by President Lincoln; however, the document was ineffective because it attempted to legalize freedom for blacks in a Confederacy that was engaged in a Civil War with the Union and; therefore, did not recognize Union governance. The 13th Amendment of 1865 abolished slavery; however, racial oppression and denial of civil liberties continued well into the 20th century. Mainstream Americans (those more likely to be conservative, republican or independent in a post-modern political era, including a significant number of successfully integrated blacks) are tired of hearing about the impact of slavery, and want very much to bury it as an event that ended in 1863. Although slavery supposedly ended 147 years ago; the damaging legacy of slavery included a colonial component, which in effect levied value estimations on blacks' souls, morality, and character. The numerical reality is that slavery did legislatively end 147 years ago but human agency exists on a continuum, which means the social construction of post civil rights blacks has just as much to do with what happened yesterday as it does a century and a half ago.

What does slavery have to do with black gangsterism? Am I suggesting that today's modern day gangbanger is gang banging because of slavery? No, what I am suggesting is that black gangsterism has a spirit of rebellion that clashes with the same democratic capitalistic society that has traditionally disenfranchised an entire class of black people in America and that these disenfranchised blacks in America are the descendants of slaves who attempted to negotiate an equitable existence in a country that was harshly opposed to their humanity. Moreover, black gangsterism is the evolved adaptation to a failed black grass roots revolution that simply did not settle the issue of injustice and inequity for marginalized black citizens. In other words where slavery ended colonialism prevailed under the disguise of integration and forced submission to marginalization, resource strain, injustice, and blocked opportunities for life course advancement.

These are significant conditions that continue to suffocate, stagnate, and perhaps overwhelm an entire class of blacks who are permanent outsiders to the functional reality of the American dream and from that we are witnessing black communities that continue to spiral into black gangland colonies ruled by criminogenic gangs in America (Cureton, 2002(a); Wilson, 1978; Frazier, 1957).

In addition to slavery, lynching was another horrific crime against blacks' humanity. Despite its uncivilized methods, lynching was considered appropriate for subhuman blacks. Raper's (1933) book *The Tragedy of Lynching* exposed the motivation for lynching. White supremacist ideology was rampant in many communities and lynching represented public executions and inter-racial regulation messages. What's more lynching also became a social spectacle. What is to be said about any group of people that takes pleasure in the inhumane death of a human being and worse what kind of Christians would consider lynching to be something to take a family to witness? Moreover, federal and law enforcement agencies rarely protected black victims from lynch mobs. It appears that church and state shared a common ground as government was slow to legislate morality and the church did very little to advance the idea that blacks shared the same covenant with God, through Jesus (specific to Christianity) and therefore, deserved humane treatment (Raboteau, 1978; Raper, 1933). Maybe the church was more concerned about not offending its congregation and; therefore, never directly challenged the inhumanity of lynching. The church can't simply choose to be relevant when it is convenient. When it mattered most (the lynching and slave era) religious institutions should have endorsed the spiritual equity of blackness but that did not happen. The counteracting message that could have given pause to blacks' inhumane treatment apparently was not firm enough to prevent blacks from having to endure another horror (lynching). Although lynching has ended, what about the social damage that it created?

What does this have to do with modern day black gangsterism? One of the more visible realities of lynching was the fact that the value placed on a black life was less than that of whites. Similarly, there is a value of life problem within the context of gangsterism as evidenced by the ease at which killing is pursued, and executed. Such a fatalistic pursuit suggests that a nihilistic germ has prevailed through generations and is now in the bloodstream of black gangsterism, which has caused them to be consciously indifferent about participating in killing campaigns. It could very well be that people who don't routinely engage in church services are not sufficiently exposed to church affirmations regarding the importance of life and in particular the importance of living a life that is pleasing to God, which could possibly explain why is it that gangs capture the hearts of males during a time when they are most vulnerable? When it matters most (for whatever reasons), the black sanctuary seems to only be a building with a powerless altar that seemingly hosts more funerals than baptisms. And the message that there is hope for redemption and that God lives, well what about it? It seems that the gangster's lifestyle is the only real sensory reality that has measurable outcomes, while God exists in faith (a seemingly untouchable leap into the unknown). Moreover, the fact that Dr. Martin Luther King's message of non-violence failed to resonate within the ghetto is evidence that reactionary behavior rooted in rebellion was favored over love and forgiveness for enemy transgressions (Hilliard, and Weise, 2002; Dawley, 1992).

CLASSISM, POLITICS AND URBANITY

Intra-racial class casting suggests that African-Americans subscribe to a five tier social caste system: (1) African-Americans who are wealthy (have net-worth value) by virtue of generational inheritance, typically the descendants of pre-emancipated blacks with land and resource ownership entitlements, or represent a highly marketable, commercialized brand that yields millions; (2) well-to-do African-Americans who earn in excess of 200,000 a year and experience the good life because of entrepreneurships, and/or those who are specialized enough to be considered an elite/owner of the mode of production in a capitalistic society; (3) the African-American middle class, a group of educated and professionally skilled people who have become integrated into a system of work and reward, earning between 90,000 to 199, 000 a year; (4) working service industry, educational agents, and/or blue collar African-Americans earning between 25, 000 to 89,000 a year and; (5) African-Americans who earn less than 10,000 a year and may be dependent upon the government for social services and living accommodations (these blacks are considered to be part of the permanent underclass or marginalized outsiders). It seems that blacks have constructed an intra-racial social ranking system based on income, prestige, educational level, resources and material acquisitions, residency and/or home value and social network groups (Wilson, 2009; West, 2001; Dyson, 1996; Anderson, 1999). An intra-racial social hierarchy suggests that permanent lower class people are deemed insignificant in terms of middle class progression in mainstream society and that they are seriously deprived and perhaps morally inferior, intellectually and culturally bankrupt enough to the point that African-Americans with earnings of at least 35,000 or more living in residential family units in community oriented neighborhoods want complete physical and mental isolation from the permanent underclass (see Wilson, 1987; Frazier 1968; Frazier 1957). This voluntary social distancing by bourgeois minded blacks has created intra-racial fear of and moral disdain for the black urban poor (West, 2001). More disturbing is the apparent nonchalant attitude regarding hope for redemption and the presence of a secret hope that those ghetto thugs, gangsters, pimps, prostitutes, drug pushers, drug abusers, and other social deviants (who seem parasitically attached to the urban underclass) will continue to engage in the type of destructive behavior that will eventually eliminate them.

How does this contribute to gangsterism? It seems logical that if blacks are likely to perceive discrimination from mainstream society, they are most certainly able to perceive and be far more hurt by black flight. Original Gangsters are fully aware that certain classes of blacks have essentially written them off as an embarrassment, and these gangsters must feel a sense of abandonment, alienation, and anger. It logically follows that gangsters would despise and reject bourgeois blacks, develop a sense of self-hate, which is a core ingredient for black-on-black victimization. A significant proportion of America, including African-Americans who have enthusiastically participated in social, economic, cultural, and spiritual black flight, are in no way passionate about the plight of the black urban poor. I offer this with regret because this intra-racial philosophy of assuming that being economically better off is equivalent to being spiritually, culturally and socially better than negates the possibility of intra-racial universal brotherhood (Cureton, 2009; Cureton, 2002(b), West, 2001; Wilson, 1987).

The political landscape for blacks was not consistently advantageous throughout various presidential administrations as evidenced by far too many Presidents doing very little to support notions of human equitability in this country. For well over a century every political gain or civil liberty advance for blacks was countered by some prohibiting and/or restrictive social code. For example, during Andrew Johnson's Reconstruction administration (1865-1869) black codes were used to counter the rights to freedom, citizenship, and voting afforded to blacks by the 13th, 14th, and 15th amendments passed in 1865, 1868, and 1870 respectively. Jim Crow laws were also used to deny blacks full citizenship rights. Additionally, the United States Supreme Court's unfavorable separate but equal rulings perpetuated racial inferiority, which contributed to the development of racially exclusive policies (Ashmore, 1997).

Nineteenth and the majority of America's twentieth century Presidents were either against, non-committal, relaxed, or provided conservative support for blacks' constitutional rights and civil protections. President Franklin Roosevelt's (1933-1945) New Deal and President Harry S. Truman's (1945-1953) Fair Deal legislation proved to be particularly vital to blacks' upward mobility and civil rights. The New and Fair Deal increased blacks' collective pursuit of civil liberties, leading to the Civil Rights Movement (1955-1970). Presidents Kennedy and Johnson's tenure (1961-1969), promoted blacks' right to civil and equitable treatment and increased civil liberties and afforded professionally trained, educated, and properly skilled blacks with opportunities. However, the movement did very little to advance the under-educated, un-employable, and socially disadvantaged masses of urban ghetto confined blacks (Wilson, 2009; Cureton, 2008; Ashmore, 1997; Wilson, 1987; Light-foot, 1968).

Despite considerable economic, social, and cultural advances and housing opportunities for blacks in a position to take advantage of them, inter-racial tension and violence remained a part of America's social climate because a significant proportion of whites across the country were threatened and envious of blacks' upward mobility and neighborhood intrusion. Presidents Nixon (1969-1974) and Reagan's (1981-1989) attitudes concerning blacks appealed to traditional southern white supremacist tradition. President Nixon's secret tapes revealed his opinion of blacks as intellectually inferior and whites as worthy of dominion over blacks. President Reagan was known to express his contempt towards the black community (Ashmore, 1997; Marable 1997; Marable 1996).Whether these personal attitudes significantly impacted their administrative decisions (relative to blacks life chances) is debatable. It could be that Presidents Nixon and Reagan's policies managed to serve the black community's interest despite their personal attitudes. Whatever the political spin, it seems that President Nixon and President Reagan's social reform policies were anti-black advancement. Particularly, President Nixon was in favor of slowing civil rights' advancements and President Reagan's policies favored the wealthy at the expense of non-whites. Upon President Nixon's resignation over Watergate, Ford's brief Presidential occupation (1974-1977) did not vary much from President Nixon's agenda.

While President elect Carter's (1977-1981) agenda overturned a period of blacks' economic, social, and cultural regression, President Reagan's brand of social reform contributed to the growth of the black underclass. Even though President George H.W. Bush (1989-1993) eventually signed the Civil Rights Bill in 1991, he vetoed it in 1990. Additionally, President George H.W. Bush used Willie Horton's infamous crime spree, while on furlough as a political platform, which effectively played on America's deep seeded contemporary fears concerning blacks' criminality. President Reagan and President George H. W. Bush's focus on black criminality and disproportionate dependence on government financial and medical assistance programs turned out to be a period of un-prosperous times and institutional targeting of lower class urban blacks (Ashmore, 1997; Marable, 1997; Marable 1996; Anderson, 1993). President Clinton (1993-2001) was embraced by the black community because he appeared to take pleasure in blacks' cultural art, music, and worship. President Clinton's favor with the black community was associated with the misplaced assumption that he was a black man trapped in white skin. However, his policies mandated more prison funding, and failed to deliver adequate economic, resource, opportunity and job surplus to inner cities across America (Robinson, 2000; Marable, 1997).

President George W. Bush's (2001-2008) tenure seemed focused on American security, social conservatism and improving energy independence. President Bush's domestic agenda relative to underclass blacks is limited to education (via the no child left behind legislation) and tax refund checks to stimulate the economy. Certainly, President Bush was partial to the core components of a progressive capitalistic society and only offered minimal concessions to the permanent underclass. Unfortunately, September 11, 2001, witnessed terrorists' attacks on New York's World Trade Centers, and Washington's Pentagon. While our democratic nation had been engulfed by unspeakable agony, universal patriotism seemed to consume the country. Americans had conceded that the perpetrators of this contemporary homeland tragedy had participated in uncivil human acts of terror. Many were looking towards our political leaders and military power for something much deeper than justice. A significant number of Americans demanded total annihilation of our enemies (identified as Osama Bin Laden, the Taliban, the Al Qaeda network, and countries that harbor terrorists). September 11, 2001, resulted in homeland insecurity and un-expected discomfort amongst most Americans, resulting in social support for our governing elite to give orders for the nation's military guards and protectors of freedom to retaliate. Except for certain anti-war groups, and/or groups promoting non-violence, patriotic Americans wanted their military to flex against terrorism. The United States' Commander in Chief, George W. Bush gave the orders and operation "Enduring Freedom" was launched on October 7, 2001, against Taliban positions in Afghanistan, twenty six days after initial terrorist attacks. Essentially, the aftermath of September's terrorists' attacks had delivered an American nation that endured the heinous offense, mourned and blessed the innocently slain, conjured the necessary emotion to move on, readied the troops, and prepared itself to embrace the 21st century's first air, water, and land campaign against homeland and international terrorism. For all of his domestic policy shortcomings, it seems that George W. Bush was an appropriate wartime President (Byman, 2008 and Phares, 2008).

Essentially then, the fairest assessment of the political landscape from 1933 through 2008 is that whatever Presidential administrations that were most beneficial to working, lower, and underclass black communities did not remain in power long enough to be comprehensively effective. On the other hand, Presidential administrations that did not favor marginalized black Americans remained in power long enough to further erode the underclass black urban community. On November 4th 2008, Senator Barack Obama became the 44th President of the United States of America. Barack Obama's victory represented a milestone in terms of the collective conscious of a voting block of Americans (regardless of color) and President Obama's victory seems to suggest that the time has come where character and merit matters more than race. However, it remains to be seen whether President Obama will develop policies that have domestic improvement implications for the permanent underclass. The United States' involvement in two wars, Iraq and Afghanistan essentially guarantees that the United States will invest money and resources to assist those countries in their post-war nation building efforts. Will we be a country that nation builds before we invest in the quality of life of our marginalized black population? The ultimate solution to black gangsterism in America rests with our ability to effectively address the seeds of discontent (i.e. economic strain and stress, limited resources, education, employment, and housing) (Cureton, 2009).

MIS-EDUCATION IS THE REAL CONSPIRACY

According to Carter G. Woodson, an educational curriculum with European standards victimizes blacks by casting them as different, deviant and pathologically opposed to a supposed universal standard that is not universal at all. In fact, the European standard inherently affords the inclusive group social dominance and the subordinate group deference to whatever set of social conditions inclusive groups deem appropriate. According to Woodson, education has been used as a weapon emphasizing the importance of integration at the expense of denouncing critical elements of blackness. A mis-educated black is dangerously exposed to an oppressive system that fails to validate his existence outside of how integrated he is in that system and once thoroughly integrated, his threat level is dismantled to the degree of being symbolically black. Arguably, education is essentially an in-doctrination to a standard that must be met in order to reach social acceptance. If this type of education negatively affects integrated blacks, what then becomes of marginalized blacks who are similarly mis-educated and perhaps under-educated (Woodson, 1933)?

There are hugely negative implications when there is too much of an emphasis placed on blacks' contentment, acceptance and/or passive assimilation relative to slavery. The most damaging being that by virtue of blacks' contentment with slavery, the slave status must have been an appropriate place for them in America's early free market economy.

What's more contentment with slavery implies that colonialism (a major component of pre and post slavery), including methods of emasculation to

decrease the threat of insurrection, were also suitable forms of indoctrina-
tion. Couple that with demonizing and criminalizing blacks' rebellion against
slavery and the end result is assassinating the character of those who did
stand up for human entitlements. History reveals that there were a variety of
adaptations to slavery. Narborough (1753), Henrietta Marie (1766), Nancy
(1769), Burla Negra (1827), Amistad (1839), and the Creole (1841) are but
a few examples of mutiny aboard slave ships. Additionally, there were an
estimated 200 to 313 slave insurrections, so to focus on the timid responses
negates the importance of masculinity for those that were resolute enough to
rebel (Meier and Rudwick, 1966; Bennett, 1962). The threat and fear level
increases with knowledge of open rebellion aboard slave ships, (where so
called superiors were overtaken and murdered) and/or knowledge concerning
the schemes and successful bloody slave revolts (e.g. Gabriel 1800, Denmark
Vesey 1822; or Nat Turner 1831). For some people it is uncomfortable to
know that there is the potential for black people to violently revoke dehumanization and servitude. Threat and fear forces the tendency to stigmatize these
actions as wicked, a-typical of humanity, and irrationally criminal. There is a
need to re-ask the question why did mutiny aboard slave ships, slave insurrections and or African survivalist attempts (African-Muslim disciplined) occur?
Could it be that these warrior/guerilla style revolts were less about murder
and more about waging war against campaigns designed to rule blackness as
indignant, infectious and not deserving of freedom (Lightfoot, 1968; Meier
and Rudwick, 1966)?

What can be gained when there is focus put on those blacks that did not
accept dehumanization or cater to being emasculated? There is something to
be gained by knowledge that African men who became American fought for
freedom and in so doing achieved masculinity that had nothing to do with
being timid. Enough, already about the house Negroes, Sambo and Uncle
Tom types, for their labels are over preached and far too common (content,
never direct, often bent over as to avoid eye contact, governed by a plantation master and one who feels humble and humiliated by a system but yet
remains grateful for whatever concessions that are afforded). Who wants to
identify with that type of person, more less that type of man? The most press-
ing problem facing young black males is attempting to negotiate manhood in
an already economic, social and culturally restrictive environment and when
you couple this with hearing about slavery in the classroom, these young
men have a natural "push back" against educational institutions (that could
potentially better their lives in the long run).

Therefore, it logically follows that when black males are exposed to historical evidence of emasculation, there will be an aggressive pursuit to transcend the weaknesses that are associated with passive resistance or perceived

indifference to human domination (slavery). The manifestation is identifying with the most accessible organization that has a clearly defined path to respectful masculinity.

The primary assumption here is that black gangsterism is significantly linked to blacks' entire racial legacy, which spans back to the continental shores of Africa and the arrival of Africans in 1619. The author contends that slavery, colonialism, lynching, as well as varying degrees of inter and intra-racial social acceptance coupled with structural inequalities and mis-education are the ingredients for black gangsterism. Some would argue the implausibility of this given landmark life course improvements overtime; however, two ingredients; horrible social conditions and the spirit of rebellion, has been consistent enough to effect post-modern blacks. There is no question that black people inherited a better society after the Civil Rights Movement and there is also no question that better does not mean equal as blacks continued to endure unfavorable civil liberties, status quo political leadership, institutionalized legal partiality, political imprisonment, federal, state, and local legal agent brutality, inept legal protections, racial tension, social rejection and indignation, and community isolation, which adversely affected blacks in general and the black urban poor in particular (Oliver, 1989; Staples 1975).

The struggle for an equitable existence entitled to citizens of this country intensified in the sixties. The sixties was a classic time where revolutionary confrontations existed on a continuum of un-conditional Christian love to passive resistance, civil disobedience through non-violent protests, to nationalistic and black power rhetoric, proactive and reactive grass roots militancy to all out person and property rebellion. In the1960's and late 1970's the opposition to a black revolution turned fatal claiming the lives of Medgar Evers (6-12-1963), Malcolm X (2-21-1965), Martin Luther King Jr. (4-4-1968), Alprentice "Bunchy" Carter (1-17-1969),Fred Hampton (12-4-1969), and George Jackson (8-21-1971). These formidable men as young as 21 and as old as 39, became martyrs to the charge for racial transcendence. They were demonized, vilified, cast as enemies to democracy, and ultimately put to death. Though I would never personally know these men, they are a part of black history. Had these men lived long enough to age into a seasoned man's life, may be the revolution would have netted wholesale progress instead of a spiraling away from black vanguards to black gangsters. A youth movement can be in step with positive components of a progressive revolution (defined as proactive and reactive steps to improve quality of life independent of government); however, what hampers the pursuit of radical change or racial transcendence is insufficient knowledge of an effective blueprint and/or the forefathers of that blueprint. The absence of true knowledge and a disciplined blueprint more than likely played some part in modern day black gangsterism (Lightfoot, 1968).

Though this book concerns black masculinity and the journey that black males have taken to prove their manhood, in all sincerity we must honor black women because they offered their sons and daughters and ultimately sacrificed a part of their souls so that the black community could receive basic freedoms. Black women gave far too much as America crucified her children even as they dared to exercise their constitutional entitlements. And let us also remember that the black woman was no idle watcher of events for she became a major ingredient for the foot soldiers known as The Black Panther Party for Self-Defense.

Chapter Two

Putting Us through Changes

Civil Rights, Black Power and the Black Panther Party for Self-Defense

The African-American experience has been confrontational and transitory because American government has proven to be a heavy handed institution of oppression and suppression in instances where government collided with black people who refused to submit to restricted access to the full entitlements of citizenship. Black people fought for basic human considerations and essentially had to rebel against a partial government that used institutional agents to criminalize political dissent. Fredrika Newton intimated that the original Black Panther Party for Self-Defense (not its contemporary version) could become a victim of misrepresentation leading to false analysis and ultimately purged from the memory of American and Black American history in spite of the evidence of the Party's existence (Hilliard and Zimmerman, 2006; Hilliard and Weise, 2002). Black scholarship should be about the business of delivering blacks' struggle for humanity to the forefront mainstream society's collective social framework as well as blacks' social conscious. If not for any other purpose but to remind all of America that whatever the historic route, nonviolent, militant, nationalist, or separatist, the goal was for blacks to have the opportunity for full participation in the American Dream and that such a pursuit should not be hindered in anyway by an agency, institutional structure, government, and/or person. Blacks have traveled a treacherous road to achieve this goal, thus, it should be no surprise that the efforts of so many had produced significant progress, and the efforts of the opposition had been successful at producing a still separate but unequal America for integrated blacks and marginalized blacks.

If we accept that race is a social construct, then race should not be thought of independently from its historical realities. Therefore, it remains critical (before levying value judgments on types of social change groups) that mainstream America develop a solid awareness of the nuances that were associated with being victims of the type of colonialism that violated every measure of blacks' physical and emotional personhood.

Long standing abuses and fatal assaults, sexual violations, denial of freedom to choose intimacy, medical experimentation with generational adverse outcomes, human trafficking, spiritual and cultural intrusions, uncertainty concerning femininity and masculinity, psychological disturbances and conflicts resulting in nihilism are but a few ingredients of colonialism that adversely impacted blacks' collective consciousness and social identity (Washington, 2006; West, 2001; Dyson, 1995; Metzger, 1971; McCarthy and Yancey, 1971; Frazier, 1968).

Whenever and wherever a government actively participates in this type of colonialism and/or fails to support blacks' human entitlements and fails to protect blacks from constitutional, legal, economic, social, and cultural victimization, what should a deserving people do about it? Movements for social change (i.e. civil rights, civil disobedience, community protest, urban resistance and disorder, black power, and black vanguards) represented different methods that attempted to address America's treatment of its black population.

Civil rights gains produced an economic, structural, political, social, cultural, and spiritual wedge between the black middleclass and the black underclass. What's more, the voice of the ghetto was politically tempered, silenced, ignored and at times, rebuked by a black leadership that seemed to be preoccupied with a middleclass integrationist agenda. The relative economic, social, cultural and spiritual comforts of integrated blacks allowed for a more patient struggle for expanded liberties, and certainly a non-violent civil approach created an aura whereby the system could be deliberately slow in its progression towards equitable entitlements (Cone, 2003; West 2001). However, the consistent deprivation associated with economic, social, and cultural marginalization produced a class of blacks that could not afford to be patient or engage in a convenient struggle. A grass roots effort had no other choice but to be aggressive, to stand in defiance and physically retaliate to relieve the pressures of oppression. It is not the case that the 60's was the most revolutionary time for black people, it represented a time when the universal brotherhood of black men segmented into those that made white people feel comfortable (the we shall overcome types marching with praise and deep faith that God would deliver) versus those that made white people fearful (black power, black fist, black control and targeted violence) (Ture, and Hamilton, 1992; and Lightfoot, 1968). The urban grass roots' black power roar was directed towards the exploits of capitalism, anti-black social regulation agents, white mainstream society, black leadership, the supposed black talented tenth, and blacks who participated in black flight. The urban voice declared that a black fist would challenge any attempts to deny their dignified existence.

The clinched fist was symbolic of a peoples' struggle, frustration, anger, and defiance regarding their disenfranchised status. Centralized in the ghetto, the brother's keeper philosophy represented unity of blood and soul brother, and the sister in the struggle with a fist prepared to deliver an equitable blow. Black Power was a movement to secure freedom and control of blacks' destiny in the ghetto and confront police misconduct and brutality. Moreover black power embodied social change whereby anti-black agents over-seeing any routine activities within the ghetto where expelled or prevented from having access to any social lifestyle events happening in the ghetto. Essentially, black power set the mood, and the Black Panthers for Self-Defense became the black fist that did the work. Can you dig it?

TO OVERCOME OR BE OVER-RUN:
CIVIL RIGHTS MOVEMENT AND BLACK POWER

Pre-civil rights concessions improving blacks' economic and social circumstances during Reconstruction era (1865-1877) were repealed, reduced, and geographically negated (in southern, northern and western states) during Presidents Ulysses S. Grant, Rutherford B. Hayes, James Garfield, and Chester Arthur's tenures (from1869 through 1885). The challengers to blacks' civil liberties and access to opportunities were northern and southern farmers, competition class whites (i.e. poor and working class whites and/or whites more likely to encounter or share the same economic, social, educational and cultural circumstances as blacks). The remainder of the 19th century (1885 through 1901) seemed to reflect an evolving unstable political landscape (populists, democrats, and republicans). Regardless of region blacks' social realities certainly were less than ideal partly because of neutral Christian religious institutions, pro-white cultural segregationists, and status quo predominantly white academic institutions. As a result, the emerging working, middle class and southern blacks who migrated north in pursuit of better economic, social, and cultural life chances found themselves in a familiar position of forced segregation, discretionary social regulation and social control, unequal access to progressive employment, education, resources, opportunity, material acquisitions, and suitable housing. The promise of an inclusive equitable America for blacks seemed to be an evasive theme and thus the struggle to seize the American dream became the 20th century, twenty one year (1954-1975) Civil Rights Movement (Geschwender, 1971; Tucker, 1968; Killian and Smith, 1960). The Christian focused, unconditional loving, accommodating, patient, compromising, non-violent, civil rights' theme, received a significant amount of media, political and mainstream journal attention because it directly casts elitist, white patriarchal groups (as the dominant groups that seemed to have their political, social and cultural interests protected by government and opportunity institutions) against a subordinate group, who by virtue of blackness were not deserving of equitable opportunity, equality before the law and assimilation into white America.

Certain segments of the American population and segregated social institutions simply did not want an integrated society, whereby black people could freely compete, socialize, and pursue a dignified lifestyle equal to that of whites (Geschwender, 1971; Meier and Rudwick, 1970; Tucker, 1968; Clark, 1966; Killian and Smith, 1960). The Reverend Dr. Martin Luther King Jr. became a martyr and champion for equity and justice for all people and yet he wondered about the unrelenting heinous treatment that blacks continued to suffer at the hands of federal, state, and local legal agents as well as competition class whites. Dr. King wondered if this country had the intestinal fortitude to rise above overt oppression given the tangible evidence that racism and discrimination had become so interwoven into America's social fabric (Cone, 2003). Economic, social employment, housing, educational and legal institutions did not stop abusing blacks because of guilt, there was no collective change of heart regarding black dignity and/or realization that black people deserved the exact same economic, social, civil, legal entitlements, educational and employment opportunities, and social accommodations. In fact there was far too much of a public outcry concerning legislating morality to think otherwise (Wilson, 2009). America was simply morally bankrupt and/or perhaps competitive enough to work the capitalistic system (including exploiting minority populations for labor and financial buying power) until it no longer became profitable to do so (Tucker, 1968).

The civil rights movement essentially represented an organized and sustained effort by churches and communities with the assistance of college and local political groups to obtain the civil privileges afforded to citizens (the right to public accommodation, education, living arrangements, employment, non-discriminatory practices in life and leisure). It was a movement with power and momentum with the goal of eliminating longstanding racial problems. The civil rights movement in many ways was a religious and spiritual approach to dealing with problems of denial, it was symbolic and transitional as it made America examine its own hypocrisy relative to freedom, bravery and creed, which were undermined by economic, cultural, political, and social discretions that failed to deliver the promise of an equitable American lifestyle. America's global reflection revealed that it was a super power that was saturated with hypocrisy in regards to politicking with blacks over civil concessions, when in reality the larger issue was human deservedness, entitlements and full engagement in a democracy (Meier and Rudwick, 1970; Clark, 1966). The American creed and practice clearly did not appear attractive and/or befitting of a nation claiming to be a moral beacon. Hence, the American democratic, free market machine became exposed and ultimately embarrassed! How could this country become an elite global entity, when the treatment of its minority populations, (well past the years of the so-called manifest destiny era) in a post-modern society rivaled that of third world developing nations?

The National Association for the Advancement of Colored People (born out of Dubois' Niagara Movement), and the National Urban League examined policies that improved conditions for blacks within the context of a democratic society, which ultimately implies that these groups where attempting to transition blacks into a middle class northern existence. Other notable civil rights, liberties, and public accommodations groups like; (1) the Congress of Racial Equality (CORE), protested the public discriminatory practices of this country; (2) the Southern Christian Leadership Conference (SCLC) (first southern civil rights groups headed by Dr. King) captured the idea that color should not be used as a basis for discrimination in any arena and this group emphasized that blacks should make adjustments; and (3) the Student Non-violent Coordinating Committee (SNCC), a group of restless young students used militant energy to non-violently protest encroachments to their civil liberties. Perhaps the most recognized collaborative action of the Civil Rights Movement was The March on Washington in 1963, which involved the SCLC, CORE, SNCC, and NAACP. Shortly thereafter the Civil Rights Act of 1964, legislation forbidding discrimination in jobs, housing, and public accommodation became the law of the land. The Civil Rights Act of 1964 mandated that law enforcement agents (like it or not) had a legal obligation to protect minorities from unfair treatment. However, there was a storm of discontent brewing amongst the poor living in northern cities, and urban areas hit hard by black flight (McCorkle and Miethe, 2002; Wilson, 2009; Wilson, 1996). Black flight, a complete economic, social, cultural, and residential distancing by middle class blacks (from communities where residents were excluded from full participation in the employment industry because of educational, vocational, and skill development deficiencies) was so devastating to those blacks left behind that communities became un-settled, collectively resource strained, fragmented and ultimately vulnerable to criminogenic subcultures and groups (Wilson, 2009; Cureton, 2009; Cureton, 2008; West, 2001; Anderson, 1999; Dyson, 1996).

Centralized misery in urban ghettos is significantly related to outbursts, revolts, rebellions, urban disorder, disobedience, and riots. It should be no surprise that destructive behaviors would somehow turn inward on community property and residents because of despair, desperation, anger, and frustration relative to blocked access to legitimate resources that provide direct access to the American dream (Sloan, 2007; Alonso, 1999; Geschwender and Singer, 1971; Meier and Rudwick, 1970; Quarantelli and Dynes, 1970; Wanderer, 1969; Tucker, 1968). An estimated 185 to 200 riots involving minority community members occurred between 1964 and 1969 and the most notable race rebellions that captured the attention of the media, increased public fear and heightened the perception that participants were blacks with higher propensities to engage in heinous crimes occurred in Chicago 1919 and 1943, Harlem 1935 and 1943, Detroit 1943 and 1967, Watts 1965, (Meier and Rudwick 1970).

> The people throwing the fire bombs now are not concerned with how many jobs the white man puts into the ghetto. They are not saying, 'give us better housing or we'll throw a bomb.' They simply want to throw a fire bomb. They want to tell society in their own way that it has placed a low premium on life in the ghetto, and the little bit of life left there they are willing to destroy to make America come to its senses (Tucker, 1968:7-8).

The unfortunate reality is that no amount of self-destructive behavior led to public sympathy and/or a call for deliberate social actions that would produce life altering changes to the ghetto. On the contrary riots that make mainstream uncomfortable translates into fear and a call for a heavy dose of regulation. History has proven that in cases where there is enough pubic fear, the use of local, state, and federal law enforcement and military might against threatening groups within the country becomes socially acceptable (Foner, 1970; Meier and Rudwick, 1970; Oberschall, 1968). Hence, riots (instead of pushing a philosophy, or forcing mainstream to accept and address frustrations related to urban misery) lead to residential victimization and property damage. Visible scars that represented the hurt and anguish was perceived as actions that were self-inflicted and un-necessary by an American public that was on the outside looking in. So the question became, what is next, what comes after inhaling the smoke from fires that came from our own community residents? The reasonable answer was to pledge solidarity to something more liberating, emancipating, hopeful and intra-community controlled than what the civil rights movement, and the Nation of Islam had been offering. Logistically situated between the civil rights movement (1954-1975) and the urban revolts (1965-1970's), black power became a movement to positively impact blacks' self-esteem and self-efficacy.

Black power meant (racial solidarity amongst the urban confined), independence, intra-community economics (generating and recycling money from black owned businesses that were sensitive to the issues of urban realities). The urban poor gravitated towards embracing individuality and separatism, instead of allegiance to America (Killian 1972: Franklin, 1969; Blauner 1962). Black Power focused on black consciousness (a divested since of self in relation to America and a re-investment in the power of African blood) and black nationalism (devotion to the development of independent and fully functional political, economic, and social institutions that make urban residency a central concern) (Ture and Hamilton, 1992; Pitts, 1974). Essentially, black power was a 1960's grass roots, (and perhaps less religiously disciplined style) reformulation of the 1920's Moorish Temple Science (initiated by Noble Drew Ali) and Garveyism/United Negro Improvement Association (founded by Marcus Garvey), which were liberation movements opposed to integration under the auspices of white dominion over blacks. Additionally, black power borrowed nationalistic principles and disciplined self-defense tactics from Minister Farrad Muhammad and Elijah Muhammad's 1930's Afro-Asian liberation movement (more commonly known as The Nation of Islam) (Lincoln, 1961).

Ultimately, black power resonated with urban residence because it identified a common enemy or cause for suffering (white), acknowledged racial equity and deservedness, racial improvement, self-reliance and the value of hard work (Meier and Rudwick 1970, Magida, 1966; Haley, 1964; Lincoln, 1961). Essentially, black power embodied a grass roots philosophy that focused on independence (from mainstream and integrated blacks) by emphasizing the importance of economic self sufficiency and political influence through registering and exercising the right to vote. However, it was the self-defense philosophy (against outside agitators, specifically the police) that appeared to be the perfect antidote for a displaced community. Black Power was more of an attitude and demeanor before it manifest as Huey P. Newton and Bobby Seal's 1966 Black Panther Party for Self-Defense (Hilliard and Weise, 2002; Foner 1970).

The ultimate fear of an American nation that had treated blacks unfairly and inhumane is that these very same blacks would develop a stronger commitment to other blacks more than identifying with the national American identity. The Black Panther Party for Self-Defense was a black vanguard group that had the passion and will to fight under a united front of deservedness. Their style was infectious and they were not bound by strict quasi religious discipline of the Moors, Garveyites, and the Nation of Islam, nor the forgiving nature of Christianity. They were the grassroots of the ghetto and there was not one assimilated black leader that could quiet their passion and voice in a manner that would comfort white America. So the Panthers were the epitome of modern day Nat Turner's, free Black Guerillas, and Melanics, in the sense that a revolt, a credible and willful opposition will be there for any white man that has the mindset to victimize the black body. The American government, law enforcement agents and the public were concerned that the Panthers were an advanced stage of legitimate black nationalism. The Black Panther Party's version of black nationalism highlighted the notion that if the current system was unwilling for (whatever reasons) to acknowledge blackness as equal, then a divorce from that system is mandatory.

What was even more dangerous about the Black Panther Party for Self-Defense was its inclusion of black women. Unlike the Civil Rights Movement, The Black Panther Party positioned black women equally. Black female Panther's were fully integrated members of the Party and engaged in the routine operations of the Party. What's more their voices were politically sharp enough to offer nuanced philosophical conversation and their fully integrated coalition with the Party also served notice that they were not afraid to honor and support the call for progressive humanity alongside other black men. Female Black Panther comrades, the likes of Kathleen Cleaver, Elaine Brown, Linda Harrison, Connie Matthews, Joan Bird, Ann Campbell, Jewel Parker, Afeni Shakur, Ericka Huggins, Patricia Hilliard, Audrea Jones, and Francis Carter-Hilliard understood the Black Panther Party to be part of a liberation movement.

Even though the Panthers were focused on addressing issues central to survival, their approach and defiance and/or failure to defer to oppressive government and abusive police officers directly cast them as political irritants, and social agitators. The most damaging effect of the Black Panther Party and in particular black women's contribution to the Party is that the public's confidence in government (its ability to offer adequate social control and regulation) waivered. The Black Panther Party for Self-Defense was viewed as a radical extremist group, which implied that the group was unreasonably fanatical and therefore predisposed to deviance, crime, and violence. The manner in which the Black Panther's image was crafted through media outlets as less intelligent (even though members of police patrols were well versed about their legal liberties and limitations) and more confrontational certainly made it easier for the public to endorse turning an American Army on black men who were acting more like a displaced colony of extremists entrenched in socialism and worse communist sympathizers. Certainly, conceptualizing the party in this manner provided fuel for J. Edgar Hoover to eliminate the party by any means necessary via declaring the party public enemy number one (Killian, 1972).

Even though the Panthers had to contend with the weight of the American government and the consequences of being labeled as criminals; Huey P. Newton (with the full understanding that legal agents would be more inclined to engage in fatalistic operations) argued that the "deep flow of play" approach, a mutual life threatening exchange, is necessary to force equitable outcomes (Hilliard and Zimmerman, 2006:46). The female comrades of the Party respected black men for their willingness to die instead of living as an emasculated man. The black female comrades understood and were effective articulators of the message that the government was engaging in political assassinations of black males made to become soldiers at war against an American institution that failed to offer the kind of liberation clearly outlined in the Declaration of Independence. These sisters in the struggle stared down the barrel of guns, dodged bullets, aimed weapons, suffered losses, fell victim to police brutality and harassment, and became public enemy number one, just like the brothers in the struggle. So many more un-named women deserve recognition and praise because they could have conveniently side stepped getting involved but instead they voluntarily became comrades in the struggle and ultimately became human shields against political bullets fired from government owned guns (Hilliard and Weise, 2002; Foner, 1970).

THE BLACK PANTHER PARTY FOR SELF-DEFENSE: BORN WITH AN IMMEDIATE EXPIRATION DATE

History has shown that mutual benefit groups have been in existence since slavery and helping blacks adjust to the hostile realities related to black citizenship in this country. Mutual benefit groups (e.g. Jones and Allen's Free African Society founded in the late 1700's to 1787, Coachman's Benevolent, Humane Mechanics, Philadelphia Library Company of Colored Persons, The Phoenix Society of New York, Brown Fellowship Society, Free Dark Men of Color, Masons and Odd Fellows, societies organized by trade, apprenticeship and specialties) emphasized independence, a resolute work ethic, self-respect, dignified living, morality, literacy, and offered economic and educational resources, medical and spiritual resources in an effort to overcome the ill effects of racism. These groups represented the earliest examples of brother's keeper organizations. However, institutional oppression and suppression, inequitable legal entitlements, alienation, marginalization, and community isolation appears to have outlasted these groups. Centuries have elapsed and the 20th century revealed that America had not come to terms with the humanity of blackness and certainly failed to reconcile the value of blackness as equal to that of whites. Social change in America moves at a snail's pace and perhaps even slower when human beings are convinced of their superiority and destiny to rule over subordinate populations. Superior groups assume confidence in human dominion and only offer concessions to subordinates when those subordinates become galvanized to protest in ways that significantly threaten social order.

The spirit of protests permeated college campuses around the country. Student protests were often university sanctioned events meaning bureaucratic protocol had to be properly satisfied before student protests could be sanctioned by the university. Of particular interests to universities was to what degree would such protests cast a negative shadow on that institution; therefore, student protest groups and/or events had to convince their respective universities that their activities would comply with rules that would not disrupt the operations of the university or adversely impact other students. There was a significant impact made by student groups who were obviously in tune with the struggle; however, too often groups like the African-American Association (AAA), Revolutionary Action Movement (RAM), and Soul Students Advisory Council (SSAC) kept their focus on improving college conditions related to course curriculums, administrator-to-student, professor-to-student, police-to-student, and student-to-student interactions. Perhaps these student groups were simply too concerned and engrossed in those activities related to their specific college that they were too exhausted to extend any meaningful action to community grass roots groups. Hence, more than anything college groups seemed more rhetorical than able to provide effective community service.

What's more the National Association for the Advancement of Colored People (NAACP), Student Non-violent Coordination Committee (SNCC), and Council of Racial Equality (CORE) denounced any organization that embraced the militancy and nationalism of black power.

Huey P. Newton and Bobby Seale were equally suspicious that the above mentioned groups ultimately desired to integrate or find ways to effectively coexist rather than challenge the oppressive nature of a money-market, capitalistic democratic institution. Newton and Seale thought that racial improvement coalitions (adult and student) were not as committed to grass roots efforts to combat ghetto conditions. However, Newton and Seale were impressed with Monroe North Carolina's NAACP chapter and The Deacons for Self-Defense because of their self-defense tactics that included firearms. Newton and Seale borrowed the panther logo from the Lowndes County Freedom Organization (LCFO) out of Alabama. The LCFO headed by Stokely Carmichael (aka Kwame Ture in 1965) was more interested in the political power of the black vote in a county that was overwhelmingly black but ruled by a minority percentage of supremacist whites.

The assassination of El Hajj Malik El Shabazz (Malcolm X; 2-21-1965) and the Watts Riot (8-11-1965) served as catalysts for the formation of the Black Panther Party for Self-Defense. The Panthers represented the spirit of Malcolm X, who spoke about the obligation to survive, and when necessary offer an intelligent reactive response that presents an equally stiff challenge to any force that intended to victimize powerless and poor black people (Hilliard and Zimmerman, 2006; Haley, 1964). In fact, this sentiment is best captured by George Jackson's statement "the point is to construct a situation where someone else will join in the dying" (Jackson, 1990:6). The Black Panther Party for Self-Defense was founded in Oakland in 1966 by Huey Newton and Bobby Seale. The Black Panther Party charged the American government with failure to protect urban poor black citizens from outright murder and police brutality. The Panthers put into action the type of reactive self-defense that Malcolm X had preached about. At least at the outset, the Panthers were beyond rhetoric and had transcended the fear of death by the gun! They were black men, black women and black youth as young as sixteen who had lived the unjust conditions of the black valley, seen the glory of the mountain top, and considered themselves deserving of better living conditions. They were not bound by the Christian agape agenda. Even if the group was destined to be terminated, the Panthers refused to yield to white men or any institution that overtly oppressed black people (Williams, 1995; McCarthy and Yancey 1971; Ladner, 1967).

The Declaration of Independence (1776) represents a decree of human rights that should not be withheld from any American citizen. The Constitution of the United States (1787-1788) represents a bill of rights that establishes the legitimacy of Americanism and individual entitlements. Essentially, the Declaration of Independence reflects a philosophical creed and the Constitution represents legislated actions designed to enhance the life course outcomes of every American citizen. However, were either of these documents originally drafted for the benefit of Africans who would become black Americans? An honest assessment of the black racial legacy in this country prompts the conclusion that Africans became American property and the American government was slow to release civil rights and human rights that were due to black people. To the extent that the founding fathers of this country could not envision an integrated society whereby blacks would be allowed to pursue their destiny free of devalued social rankings, then the Declaration of Independence nor the Constitution was designed for the benefit of Africans who would become black American citizens. Alternatively, to the extent that the founding fathers did envision a time when all men would be treated equally, then the Declaration of Independence and the Constitution was written for the benefit of all American citizens regardless of color.

When in the course of human events, it becomes necessary for one people to dissolve the political bonds which have connected them with another, and to assume, among the powers of the earth, the separate and equal station to which the laws of nature and nature's God entitle them, a decent respect to opinions of mankind requires that they should declare the causes which impel them to the separation....We hold these truths to be self-evident, that all men are created equal; that they are endowed by their Creator with certain inalienable rights; that among these are life, liberty, and the pursuit of happiness. That, to secure these rights, governments are instituted among men, deriving their just powers from the consent of the governed; that, whenever any form of government becomes destructive of these ends, it is the right of the people to alter or abolish it, and to institute a new government, laying its foundation on such principles, and organizing its powers in such form, as to them shall seem most likely to effect their safety and happiness. Prudence, indeed, will dictate that governments long established should not be changed for light and transient causes; and, accordingly, all experiences hath shown, that mankind are more disposed to suffer, while evils are sufferable, than to right themselves by abolishing the forms to which they are accustomed. But, when a long train of abuses and usurpations, pursuing invariable the same object, evinces a design to reduce them under absolute despotism, it is their right, it is their duty, to throw off such government, and to provide new guards for their future security (Declaration of Independence, 1776 and see Hilliard and Weise, 2002:57).

A classic 20th century war involving federal, state and local social control institutions versus a grass roots black vanguard group was on the horizon. From initial arrival to the Americas in 1619 through the 1960's and arguably better times in 1970 (approximately 351 years), it appears that blacks racial life chances suffered because of slavery, colonialism, black codes, Jim crow, overt and covert racism, discrimination, oppression, and suppression, social and educational inequality, discretionary justice, differential access to opportunities for advancement, resource strain and neighborhood isolation, which fundamentally implies that America had declared war on blacks in general and poor powerless blacks in particular. The militant leaders who spearheaded black nationalism, and black power were in many ways opposed to the pitfalls of democracy. Perhaps this explains why the Black Panther Party endorsed or aligned itself with socialism/communism, which was seen as anti-American, when it was actually anti-colonialism. It was an opportunity to resist selective integration and promote forging opportunities for blacks to demonstrate their intelligence, self-governing ability, mechanical talents (Blauner, 1969; Woodson, 1933).

The Panthers were organized around a Ten Point platform, that both Newton and Seale thought represented the spirit of a freedom in America. Fundamentally, the Panther's social change platform embodied the freedom to determine social destiny within the black community, and end capitalistic exploitation of the black community. Additionally, the Party politicked for; (1) decent housing, education, and gainful employment; (2) exemption from military service; (3) an immediate end to police brutality and murder; (4) the release of black persons in prison who are there by virtue of discretionary justice; (5) jury trials with like circumstanced blacks; and (6) freedom to determine national destiny and the right to live in peace (Hilliard and Zimmerman 2006, Foner 1970). The Panther's 10 point "want" platform was matched by their 10 point "belief" system. The first two wants (desiring freedom to control the economic and social realities of the ghetto and full access to the employment industry) and beliefs (the ability to determine destiny is the true mark of freedom and that the federal government is obligated to provide gainful employment or provide monetary compensation in order to improve social living conditions) did represent the spirit of America: however, the want platform was more independent and the belief platform seemed more dependent on government employment or money concessions. The third want (to end government exploitation of the black community) and belief (the government is fundamentally racist and is entitled to provide economic reparations to the black community), reflects the wants and beliefs of alienated Americans and in some ways very much anti-American because of the stance that the American government is corrupt, racist and has an overdue debt to repay to powerless blacks.

The fourth and fifth wants (decent shelter and an Afro-centric education) and beliefs (fair housing is made possible by housing cooperatives controlled by black people and education should be inclusive of how America has been disloyal to black Americans throughout history) is partly pro-American in terms of residential independence and understanding the value of education but is simply unrealistic in terms of asking for the type of education that reveals America's awful history of human and civil rights violations. The sixth and seventh wants (exemption from military service and an end to police abuse, harassment, brutality and murder) and beliefs (that it is not practical to soldier for a racist government that similarly victimizes minority populations around the world and adherence to the constitutional right to become armed for purposes of self-defense) is partly pro-American in terms of a desire to adhere to constitutional entitlements but more ant-American and unpatriotic to rebuff the call to become soldiers and/or willingly engage in proactive assaults on police officers. The eighth and ninth wants (the release of incarcerated black men deemed political prisoners and like circumstanced blacks serving on legal juries in cases where blacks are on trial) and beliefs (the discretionary practices of the legal system has proved impartial towards blacks and impartial nature of jury trials can be reversed if the 14th Amendment to the Constitution was honored in its purest form) platform is strictly an American guarantee related to fair processing within the legal system. The tenth want (a separate black colony, completely divested from white governance) and belief (that a separate state of equitable functionality was warranted given America's long history of human abuses directed at black people) represents American idealism. It is certainly American to want to be divested from oppressive regimes but anti-American to expect an American government to honor the request for separation with land, economic, educational and material resources (Hilliard and Zimmerman, 2006; Hilliard and Weise, 2002; Foner 1970). Even though the Black Panther Party for Self-Defense represented a mixed bag of American ideals and principles with anti-American sentiments, its militant confrontational style virtually guaranteed that the organization would become so threatening that it would soon be declared the number one internal threat to American security.

> Prudence, indeed, will dictate that governments long established should not be changed for light and transient causes; and, accordingly, all experiences hath shown, that mankind are more disposed to suffer, while evils are sufferable, than to right themselves by abolishing the forms to which they are accustomed. But, when a long train of abuses and usurpations, pursuing invariable the same object, evinces a design to reduce them under absolute despotism, it is their right, it is their duty, to throw off such government, and to provide new guards for their future security (Declaration of Independence, 1776 and see Hilliard and Weise, 2002:57).

The appeal of socialism and communism was that it convicted America, casting it as a country of hypocrisy and irrational thought for suggesting that democracy has as a core value equitable treatment. Communist governments exploited blacks by appearing to offer sympathy for their life course condition as economically, socially, and culturally oppressed.

America had been exposed and positioned on a global stage where it would be nationally shamed and labeled delusional for promoting democracy over socialism or communism (Hilliard and Zimmerman, 2006; Meier and Rudwick, 1966). The Panther's rational for adopting or at least flirting with communism was an effort to ideologically flush out the racism that is inherently a fixture of a capitalistic structure; however adopting such a philosophy was taken as a war declaration against Americanism. Hence, The Black Panthers and any other leader thought to be sympathetic to communism were considered grossly un-patriotic and treasonous. Subscribing to socialism or communism was like siding with oppositional countries during World Wars I (Germany, Austria, Bulgaria) and II (Germany, Italy, Japan) (Hilliard and Zimmerman 2006). Additionally, the fact that the Black Panther Party seemed to endorse any ideology associated with America's Cold War foe, the Soviet Union, openly criticized the Vietnam War, engaged in political discourse with Fidel Castro, took up refuge in places like Cuba and South America and applauded the legitimacy of notable revolutions and revolutionaries in Africa, Korea and Japan had the appearance of the Party trying to directly undermine America's political system. There is a difference between exercising the right to political dissent and endorsing communist lead revolutions and/or liberation movements. In defense of the Black Panthers, the amount of frustration associated with wholesale marginalization coupled with law enforcement abuse more than likely forced a political distancing from America that ultimately landed too close to communism. Perhaps government agencies charged with the duty to maintain domestic tranquility were rightfully concerned that the grass roots population, specifically the disenfranchised black urban-underclass male was predisposed to subscribe to national threat philosophies (communism, socialism/all taken to mean a re-distribution of the modes of production to effect a better positioning of the collective or masses) that ran counter to American democracy.

J. Edgar Hoover's administration lasted from 1924 to 1972. He was considered the most powerful law enforcement agent for well over 45 years. No matter the political language, the evidence is clear that Hoover's style of social regulation received consistent approval given Hoover served under eight Presidential administrations (Presidents: Calvin Coolidge, Herbert Hoover, Franklin D. Roosevelt, Harry S. Truman, Dwight Eisenhower, John F. Kennedy, Lyndon B. Johnson and Richard Nixon), four of which (Presidents; Eisenhower, Kennedy, Johnson and Nixon) witnessed Hoover's relentless attack on black social change groups during the 1960's.

Hoover's FBI tactics were effective enough to neutralize most organizations that he aggressively pursued and the Black Panther Party for Self-Defense was no exception. J. Edgar Hoover went after Dr. Martin Luther King Jr, Malcolm X, The Nation of Islam and the Black Panthers using government approved agencies who had clearances to side-step constitutional protections (i.e. wiretaps, no warrant entries, create perception of disunity, disharmony, and distrust via stigmatizing and falsely labeling members as informants, supplying financial documents, forging letters and correspondence, etc.). The Nation of Islam emerged as the only resilient group that had the power to withstand the weight of the government, even though it had lost its most prolific messenger, Minister Malcolm X.

The Black Panther Party could not survive the Federal Bureau of Investigations (FBI), Central Intelligence Agency (CIA), Drug Enforcement Agency (DEA), Internal Revenue Service (IRS), Bureau of Narcotics and Dangerous Drugs (BNDD), Alcohol, Tobacco and Firearms Division, Bureau of Customs, Law Enforcement Assistance Administration (LEAA), Office of Drug Abuse Law Enforcement (ODALE), State Department of Justice (SDJ), Organized Crime and Criminal Intelligence Branch (OCCIB) who were in collusion at the local, state and federal level. Whether separate from or an umbrella organization to the COINTELPRO operation, the goal was to destroy the Black Panther Party. These institutional government agencies felt completely justified in challenging and suppressing black nationalists groups using any method necessary as long as such actions could not be directly linked to the bureau in a manner that would cause social embarrassment. Government officials felt that communism represented an extreme agitation to American democracy and could therefore fuel a revolutionary subculture of violence aimed at the American government.

TERMINATING THE PARTY THE OLD FASHION WAY

Hoover's objective was to transform the Panthers' political opposition into a movement of criminals and social terrorist that were of no value to mainstream America and black America for that matter. The best way to achieve this goal was to criminalize the Panther's most routine activities, force them into being an economic liability to the community, and engage in a public campaign to discredit their actions and cast them as a negative element that forces police to intrude upon the peace of the community more so than they were already accused of doing. Essentially, under Hoover's FBI administration COINTELPRO condoned tactics (fraud, fudging evidence, deceit, entrapment, discretionary justice, impartial attention, police harassment, profiling, baiting, trumped up legal challenges related to drug trafficking, weapons violations, extortion, narcotics use, and gangsterism) designed to divide, conquer, and weakened what was perceived to be a dangerous black political group. Ultimately, the communities that the Panthers were organized to serve would be the same communities that would expel them (Hilliard and Weise, 2002; Garrow, 1981).

Hoover simply exposed the brother's keeper philosophy (originating out of early Negro schools of thought; Tuskegee Institute, National Urban League, Negro improvement associations, and Radical Nationalists groups, Booker T. Washington and W. E. B. Dubois, Dubois and Marcus Garvey) as nothing more than rhetoric. History has shown that even though blacks have had the exact same goal of eliminating unfavorable life course conditions there has been a consistent rivalry amongst the leadership, enough to derail social change (i.e. NAACP versus UNIA, Christian Non-Violent Movements versus The Nation of Islam, student protest groups versus grass roots black power community groups, Revolutionary Action Movement and Ron Karenga's Organization US, versus the Black Panthers, Dr. King versus Malcolm X and Cleaver versus Newton) (Hilliard and Zimmerman, 2006; Hilliard and

Weise, 2002; Foner, 1970; Meier and Rudwick, 1970). Unfortunately, the easiest route to the Panthers' destruction was to plant seeds of distrust, which quickly led to dissention and the deterioration of the Black Panther Party for Self-Defense. A variety of supposedly authentic police, FBI and even Panther memorandums were used to plant faulty information and misinformation calling into question the credibility, honesty and trustworthiness/solidarity of black leadership within the organization and the black community.

Hoover, still had one major problem and that was that the Panther's militant style, dress code, demeanor and open display of weapons appealed to young urban youth because the organization seemingly provided a channel for expressing anger and frustration. Youth were particularly attracted to the Panthers because of an absence of a strict religion. Newton understood all too well (probably because he knew to turn to the streets to recruit) that black youth would be attracted by a successful vanguard group who provided a reputable challenge and was able to openly rebuke the cruel intentions of oppression in front of an audience right there on their own turf (the streets, the hood's version of the stage)(Foner, 1970). This perceived level of youthful admiration for the Panther Party offers a clear cut rational for why local law enforcement agencies were instructed to destroy the food supply the Panther's used for its breakfast program. Stated another way, legal agents perceived the breakfast program as less of a noble community effort and more of an opportunity to indoctrinate a new generation of Panthers. How could a federal institution pacify an entire generation of potential new Black Panthers?

The end game is that the original version of the Black Panther Party was effectively rendered inoperable in 1969 and Huey P. Newton was murdered in 1989. Newton was forty-seven years old. Arguably it was a mistake to subscribe to communism, socialism, nationalism and afrocentrism as these doctrines made enemies more so than promoted social change. Although, the Panther Party was successful in garnering respect, restoring masculinity to the ghetto by winning some street battles against local police officers, and effectively dealt with morning hunger through its breakfast program, the Party failed to bring about change in the ghetto.

> Settle your quarrels, come together, understand the reality of our situation, understand that fascism is already here, that people are dying who could be saved, that generations more will die or live poor butchered half-lives if you fail to act. Do what must be done, discover your humanity and your love in revolution. Pass on the torch, join us, give up your life for the people (Quote by George Jackson, 1994:xxv).

In the final analysis, democracy rules, the ghetto continues to deteriorate, and have its economic power siphoned away, police continue to openly abuse marginalized populations, and middle class blacks remain at an untouchable distance. What's more maybe the government turned away from its responsibility (yet again) to protect citizens from harm by loosening restrictions that led to flooding the community with criminogenic vices related to a drug economy. The irony now is that the children that the Panther Party proudly served breakfast to are now feeding off of gangsterism and their gangster lifestyle is the only tangible evidence that the Panthers ever existed.

Chapter Three

The Farmer's Harvest

Fertile Land for African-American Gangsterism

Street hustling and gangsterism appears to represent the pursuit of human dignity, respectability, and manhood in deprived and morally conflicted environments. Essentially, it appears that when black males become fully cognizant of their marginalization they respond by subscribing to a gangster counter-culture imbedded in nihilism, juvenocracy, rebellion and a gangster's creed. This chapter explores how manhood is negotiated, achieved and maintained within the context of social change at the community level. The conceptual framework is the Emergent Gangsterism Perspective (EGP), which attempts to offer some insight relative to the emergence of black street gangs in most urban cities. This perspective fundamentally assumes that ganglands evolved from four community transitional stages: defined community (stage 1:1920-1929); community conversion (stage 2: 1930 to 1965); gangster colonization (stage 3: 1966-1989); and gangster politicalization (stage 4: 1990 and well into the 21st century).

Institutional stratification and unequal access to human and civil liberties, rights and affordances has significantly altered black males' quest for functional citizenship and respectable manhood (Wilson, 2009; Knox, 2009; Cureton, 2008; Anderson, 1999; Williams, 1995; Metzger, 1971; Keegan, 1968). A significant segment of black men have had to contend with a history of inhumane oppression and opportunity blockages, social, and cultural rejection, and isolation, which distorted their passage to manhood (Knox, 2009; Cureton, 2008; Dyson, 2000; Magida, 1996; Taylor, 1990; Oliver, 1989; Haley, 1964; Frazier, 1957).

NUMERICAL ILLUSIONS AND
HOOD DYNAMICS FOR BOYZ TO BECOME MEN

An often cited statistical fact concerning the relationship between race and the criminal justice system is that blacks are disproportionately represented in both the criminal justice and juvenile court system. Disproportionate representation implies over-representation in that even as blacks are a minority in the U.S. population 12.3% to 12.8 % (between 36 to 40 million) of approximately 305 million people in the United States, their incarceration percentage is estimated at 47% (or nearing 1 million) of the total 2.3 million prisoners. The case for black youth is that they comprise approximately 15% of the population under the age of 18 but make up 45% of detainees. Putting this in perspective, there are approximately 66 million black and white youth under the age of 18 in the U.S. population (11 million are black and 55 million are white). The estimated population of juveniles being serviced by the juvenile court system is between 2.2 and 3 million.

If black juveniles are detained in the system at 45% (much higher than their population representation of 15%) then black juveniles make up roughly 1.2 million of 3 million detained juveniles in the court system. A straight forward percent analysis suggests over-representation of black adults and black juveniles (population representation versus court system representation) (Gabbidon and Greene 2009; Bureau of Justice Statistics 2009, Office of Juvenile Justice and Delinquency Prevention Statistics 2009, United States Census Bureau Quick Facts 2009, and World Facts, Populations Statistics, 2008). However, the problem with this one-sided statistical representation is that it evokes the image of blacks as the symbolic assailant for crimes involving serious person-to-person and street crimes, which manifests as social panic over blacks' criminality (Walker, Spohn, and Delone, 2007; Markowitz and Jones-Brown, 2000). An alternative statistically true; and therefore, equally as relevant straight forward numerical assessment reveals that out of 36 to 40 million African-Americans in the United States, roughly 1 million are adult prisoners and 1.2 million of the 11 million African-Americans under the age of 18 are considered juvenile delinquents. Granted 1 million adult prisoners and 1.2 million detained juveniles are causes for concern, there are still between 33 to 38 million African-Americans who have not been classified as adult criminals or juvenile delinquents, which means that African-Americans largely subscribe to law abiding, functional citizenship (Bureau of Justice Statistics 2009, Office of Juvenile Justice and Delinquency Prevention Statistics 2009, United States Census Bureau Quick Facts 2009, and World Facts, Populations Statistics, 2008).

A demographic profile of criminals suggests that socioeconomic status, family dynamics, gender, age, and urbanity are significant predictor variables for deviance, crime and violence (Gabbidon and Greene 2009; Agnew, 2005; Short, 1997; Gottfresdon and Hirschi, 1990; Wilson and Herrnstein, 1985). A fundamental assumption of this chapter is that the 2.2 million black adult and juvenile inhabitants of America's penitentiary warehouses were more likely (than not) to be exposed to the adverse circumstances related to residency in resource strained, economic, cultural, and socially deprived urban area (Wilson, 2009; Cureton, 2008; Williams, 2004; Wilson, 2002; West, 2001; Anderson, 1999; Dyson, 1996; Wilson, 1996; Anderson 1990; Wilson, 1987; Keegan, 1971; Wanderer, 1969; Tucker, 1968). Therefore, there appears to be a need to re-address the nature and meaning of black masculinity within the context of race and class specific situational life course circumstances for the sake of arriving at a better understanding of black masculinity within the ghetto.

Ruth Benedict asserts "the life history of the individual is first and foremost an accommodation to the patterns and standards traditionally handed down in his community. From the moment of his birth the customs into which he is born shape his experience and behavior. By the time he can talk, he is a little creature of his culture, and by the time he is grown and able to take part in its activities, its habits are his habits, its beliefs his beliefs, its impossibilities his impossibilities" (Benedict; 1934:2-3).

It logically follows that within the black ghetto, masculinity would be differentially experienced because of varying degrees of deprivation, marginalization, isolation, and community exposure to violence (Viosin and Guilamo-Ramos, 2008; Agnew, 2005; Williams 2004; Anderson, 1999; Wilson, 1996; Wilson, 1987; Pitts, 1974). The Emergent Gangsterism Perspective (EGP) posits that gangsterism emerged as a counter-culture to blocked access to social legitimacy within mainstream culture. Gangsterism is the process of becoming a gangster (a ghetto superstar by virtue of deviant, criminal and violent predation). Becoming a respectable gangster is equivalent to achieving an ultimate measure of ghetto manhood (Cureton, 2008; Williams, 2004; Shakur, 1983).

Eldridge Cleaver prophetically proclaimed "we shall have our manhood, we shall have it or the earth will be leveled by our attempts to gain it" (Cleaver; 1968:84). According to Cleaver, neither the confines of a depressed ghetto or the restrictions of incarceration are strong enough to force men to give up their pursuit of social legitimacy. In fact, for Cleaver whenever conditions become overly oppressive the pursuit of manhood becomes a dangerously destructive journey. Stated another way, regardless of the condition, the challenge of men is to matter on some level, and black men, will find a way to matter in a world that implies that they have no value. Perhaps Cleaver offered a key ingredient to gangsterism by hinting at the destructive activities that frustrated black men would intentionally pursue in route to masculine entitlements.

The American Dream has bypassed a significant portion of blacks, which has resulted in a permanent underclass of people residing in two distinct environments: (1) ganglands or hood enclaves where street gangs have become the primary agent for those seeking ghetto superstardom (neighborhood respect, street credibility, monetary gain and material acquisition); and (2) government subsidized low income housing areas (the projects) where cliques of block hustlers (drug dealers and thugs ready to employ violence to settle disputes) dominate the scene (Cureton, 2008; Cureton, 2002; West, 2001; Anderson, 1999; Short, 1997; Wilson, 1996; Wilson, 1987; Anderson, 1990).

In response, black male residents embrace and engage in an alternate employment industry that promotes getting money and elaborate lifestyle symbols (i.e. cars, clothes, jewelry, and women) through drugs, gun trafficking, prostitution, gambling, stolen property, street racing, and dog-fighting. Embracing what appears to be a criminogenic subculture mandates street politicking, overt displays of aggression, fighting, and often the use of lethal violence to resolve social conflicts and in so doing the more successful males ultimately become reputable gangsters (Cureton, 2008; Stewart and Simons 2006; Stewart, Schreck and Simons, 2006; Williams, 2004; Cureton, 2002; Shakur, 1993; Anderson, 1999; Anderson, 1990; Katz, 1988; Cloward and Ohlin, 1960; Miller, 1975; Miller, 1958; Cohen, 1955).

BRIEF HISTORY OF BLACK GANGSTER FORMATIONS

I do pledge allegiance to my flag within the ghetto of the United States of America, and to the hood for which it stands one gang-set under the sun, invincible with righteous living and street justice for all.

Residents of inner cities in this country are dying of thirst and the water burns the throat with each attempt to swallow, leaving behind nothing but inner city blues. There is no time and there is no need to listen to conventional clichés arresting attempts at survival and reducing lifestyle choices to pathological exploits with self inflicted crippling consequences. There simply is a shortage of advantages, affordances, allowances, and privilege. Nothing comes to sleepers but a dream and dreams become hopeless time travels quickly dashed by gritty water that forces the burning eye to witness the daily nightmare. Ghetto living is trying to avoid dying before finding meaning. The ghetto is a place where the spirit is amputated, the soul executed, and the flesh becomes a human shield with internal injuries related to shame. Yet in these black colonies so commonly known as ghettos across this expansive country, gangs have become refuge and gangsterism, salvation. The formation of street corner subcultures and gangs in most major urban areas (i.e. South Central, Los Angeles, Chicago, Philadelphia, New York, New Jersey, Baltimore, Florida and Texas) and even smaller predominantly black socially disorganized neighborhoods (i.e. Ohio, Connecticut, North and South Carolina; Arkansas, Mississippi, New Orleans, Kentucky, Kansas, Oregon, Portland, and Seattle) is significantly related to consistent struggles to overcome structural and social oppression and suppression, the relative success of the Civil Rights Movement (e.g. black flight, community declination, inequity and unequal access to life enhancing opportunities), blacks' migration and urban population density, discretionary justice and coercive policing, negative labeling, public scorn, differential access to legitimate opportunities, dysfunctional family dynamics, inept parenting, community isolation, a subculture of deviance, crime, and violence in addition to access to the drug and gun underground economy (Cureton, 2008: Sloan, 2007; Anderson, 1999; Cureton, 1999; Anderson, 1990; Hagedorn, 1988; Wilson, 1987). Black street gangs have traditionally been a product of most underclass communities and the evidence on black gangsterism reveals that gangs represent a response to oppression, isolation, resource strain, deprivation, denial of rights and freedoms, and blocked access to economic and social legitimacy. The black gang phenomenon often gets reduced to a criminogenic enterprise in spite of the fact that black gangs were at times civil enough to assist in the struggle for equality and were accepted as positive organizations for social change. For example, Crips, Vice Lords and Disciples were endorsed as positive community organizations by local political leadership in the 1970's; while Vice Lords, P-Stones/El Rukins were thoroughly integrated enough to secure government grants, and purchase real estate property that became central command posts for community improvement social programs. Unfortunately, the civility and perhaps altruistic noble efforts for social change and community improvement just simply could not survive federal, state and local governments' legitimate and illegitimate practices, police officers' discretionary practices, and the lure of urban temptations related to hustling, gambling, running numbers, pimping, prostitution, and drugs (Cureton, 2008; Sloan, 2007; Knox, 2004 (a); Shakur, 1993; Short and Strodtbeck, 1965; Golding, 1954). Essentially, black gangs are products of marginalization and isolation from the routine practices related to functional citizenship and denied access to full participation in the money market culture of America. What's more black street gangs emerged from close knit familial brotherhoods and neighborhood crews, cliques and posses. These groups became integrated defense and/or conflict groups because of societal rejection, and social conflict with other ethnic street gangs. Moreover, these defense groups evolved into criminal gangs, once similarly circumstanced males internalized the effects of marginalization and immediately embraced principles promoting deviance, crime, and/or violence as options to transcend resource strain and material deprivation.

The origins of Chicago's contemporary super predator street gangs can be traced to the rapid transition of traditionally white neighborhoods to black (between 1917 and 1920). Inter-racial conflict between white youth gangs, who were fighting for segregationist principles (i.e. Canaryville Bunch, The Almighty Gaylords, Lorraine Club, Aylward Club, Pine Club, Emeralds, Favis Greys, Mayflower, Hamburgs, Ragens Colts, and Studs Lonigan) and street corner black males, who were fighting for the freedom to associate in otherwise racially restricted areas (i.e. Jewtown, Egyptian Cobras, Racketeers, Chaplains, Imperial Chaplains, Roman Saints, Nobles, Mafia, Vampires, Braves, Navahoes, and Sioux) (Dawley, 1992, Short and Strodtbeck, 1965; Thrasher, 1927) were common.

Essentially, inter-racial social conflict related to territorial claims over streets, alleys, railroad tracks, storefronts, building stoops and small waterfronts were enough to transition otherwise neighborhood groups into serious street gangs (Thrasher, 1927).

The Devil's Disciples, P-Stones and Vice Lords were the three major street organizations that were formed in Chicago during the latter years of 1950 and early 1960's. The Vice Lords (1958) and the Black P-Stone Nation/Black Stone Rangers (1959) were formed in the Illinois State reformatory school at Saint Charles (Knox and Papachristos, 2002; Dawley, 1992). Peppilow was one of the original founders of the Vice Lords, and Fort and Hairston were co-founders of The Black P. Stone Nation. The P-Stone Nation would eventually become a gang empire known as the Nation of Brothers (i.e. umbrella organization for Gangster Stones, Jet Black Stones, Rubes, Future Stones, P.R. Stones, and Corner Stones) (Knox 2004(a); Short and Strodtbeck, 1965). Abdullah-Malik (formerly Fort) transitioned from P-Stone to El Rukn, which was an organization with an Islamic focus. The El Rukn gang is most infamous for allegedly agreeing to become foot-soldiers for Libya's Moamar Khadafy in exchange for an estimated 2.5 million dollars (Knox, 2004(a)).The Devil's Disciples gang was formed in 1960 and splintered into three warring factions between 1960 and 1973: (1) Barksdale "aka" King David's Black Disciples (BD's); (2) King Hoover's Black Gangster Disciples (BGD's); and (3) members of the Supreme Gangsters became the Gangster Disciples (GD's). The rift between Black Disciples and Black Gangster Disciples and brutal alliances with the Folk Nation (constellation of Spanish speaking gangs) who are adversaries with the People Nation (constellation of

Spanish speaking, Latin, and Black Gangs) stretches to Gary, Indiana, and Milwaukee. These gangster alliances are in many ways superficial enough to nurture dissention and perhaps solid enough to fuel decade long feuds (Knox, 2004(b); Knox, 2004(c); Knox and Fuller 2004).

The Gang Capital of America is South Central Los Angeles and in similar fashion to the proliferation of gangs in Chicago, South Central's (now known as South, Los Angeles) Crip and Blood gangs originated from leisurely associations of neighborhood boys. The transition to street fighting groups was the result of community opposition, inter-racial peer group conflict and eventually intra-racial competition (Thrasher, 1927). The migration of blacks to white and immigrant communities in Southern Los Angeles began with the freedom train, Argonaut Express, which transported New Orleans and Mississippi blacks to neighborhoods settled by Italian, German, Lithuanian, Russians, Armenian, Croatian, and Serbian groups. However the more severe physical opposition came from Spook Hunters (white youth vanguard groups) as their behaviors were more representative of racial hate crimes.

Hailing from the deep-south black males understood the proven strategy of collective action and collective brotherhoods. Slausons, Farmers, Businessmen, Gladiators, Watts Gang, and Devil Hunters represented vanguard groups in defense of perceived social entitlements (the main one being, not being harassed, victimized or intimidated by white youth). Essentially, early brotherhoods (lasting from 1940 until the mid 1960's) where liberators and pioneers; however, the social gains won by these groups were short lived because the weight of structural oppression (i.e. community crowding, strained resources, physical and social deprivation) eventually led to residential frustrations and urban unrest (i.e. 1965 Watts Riots) (Cureton 2008; Sloan, 2007; Alonso 1999; Gesehwender, 1971).

There were essentially two young adult movements, one entrenched in Black Power and the Black Panther Party for Self-Defense and the other represented those youth who became disgruntled that the Panther Party had seemingly failed to deliver on the promise of improving the ghetto. The Black Panther Party for Self Defense established in 1966 by Bobby Seale and Huey P. Newton directly confronted civil inequity, social injustice and police brutality and attempted to address the underground economy and black victimization (Foner, 1970). Alprentice "Bunchy" Carter (informally regarded as mayor of the ghetto and one whom many consider to be the most influential urban leader for a youth liberation movement) became the president of the Panthers' Los Angeles chapter (Sloan, 2007; Alonso, 1999; Foner, 1970). The Federal Bureau of Investigation quickly designated the Black Panthers a street terrorist organization and launched the Cointelpro campaign to eliminate the group. Unfortunately, the FBI was extremely effective at criminalizing the Panthers and effectively rendering the movement stagnant by incarcerating the leadership. Eventually, the Panthers' were neutralized as a direct result of J. Edgar Hoover's counterintelligence program. The liberation movement was often left in the capable hands of female comrades and unfortunately the street detail was landed in the hands of urban youth who were not prepared to assume leadership (Magida 1996; Foner, 1970; Cleaver, 1968). Disappointed with the Panther Party's inability to endure government attacks, Alprentice "Bunchy" Carter sensed the disappointment coming from the youth and he attempted to harness that energy; however his blueprint for success would never be fully carried out because he was murdered on the campus of UCLA in 1969.

Alprentice "Bunchy" Carter was about eleven years older than Raymond Washington and Stanley "Tookie" Williams and these two became the next generation to assume the reins of community street power, and the organization designated to assume that power was the Crips (Common Revolution In Progress or Community Revolutionary Inter-Party Service, Cradle to the Grave Rest In Peace, CRYPT from Tales from the Crypt, KRYPTS from Kryptonite, and Baby Avenues to CRIBS—although it is debatable whether these names ever officially were acronyms for the Crips) (Cureton, 2008; Sloan 2007; Williams , 2004; Knox, 2000; Alonso, 1999; Shakur, 1993). Washington and Williams' alliance seemed to concentrate on criminogenic opportunities related to gangster territorial claims, drug (marijuana, phencyclidine pill–pcp, and heroin) and gun (uzis, ak-47's and colt ar-15 assault rifles) trafficking and control. Street gang feuds began to dominate the social scene as the Crips' supposed omnipotent gangster appeal did not sit well with neighborhoods that did not identify with Crip. Even though neighborhood after neighborhood united and became a branch of the Crip Empire (i.e. Rollin 20's through 60's, Hoover, Eight Tray Gangsters, Grape Street, East and West Side, Avalon Garden, Shot Gun, Kitchen, Compton, Venice, etc.,), Athens, Brims, Bishops, Bounty Hunters, Denver Lanes, Pirus, and Swans would organize to become the Blood gang (1973-1975). The Blood philosophy was that a far more ruthless approach was mandatory to overcome being out-numbered by the Crips (Sloan, 2007; Alonso, 1999). Crips and Bloods battled for money, power and respect and unfortunately fatal violence became the ultimate negotiating tactic. The Crip and Blood feuds are historic and the final analysis suggests that whatever influence the Black Panther Party, Slausons, Farmers, Businessmen and Gladiators once had has diminished and has been replaced by a death campaign.

The brief history of black street gangs is certainly not exhaustive by any means. There is no question that there are far too many pockets of deprivation in urban and rural areas that have some type of street corner network attached to it. Moreover, females certainly have a history in black gangsterism as either independent (Holly Ho's and Queen Bees), auxiliary (Vice Queens), or integrated (Cripettes, Bloodettes, Hooverettes etc.) members. Female gangsterism, particularly those who engaged in enough deviant, criminal and violent work in order to achieve crazy bitch or female original gangster status deserves as much recognition as the male gangs presented here (Brown, 1999; Fishman, 1999; Fishman, 1995). Unfortunately, the nature and extent of female involvement in gangsterism is beyond the scope of this book given the focus is on masculine adaptations to adverse structural, economic, social, and cultural conditions. Additionally, the brief history presented here is not intended to slight black gangsterism in Detroit, where the infamous Black Mafia Family (founded by Demetrius and Terry Flenory, "Big Meech" and "Southwest T," respectively) put in enough work to become a notable gang in history.

The Harlem numbers game produced organized crime where black organized gangs seized control of running numbers, gambling, pimping, extortion, and fencing, as well as going to war with non-black ethnic organized crime groups.

The black convict is America's criminal reality and is warehoused in institutional facilities where civility, peaceful relations and universal brotherhood are contingent upon allegiance to street gangs that have become institutionalized, and/or prison gangs with an Islamic, black power or black nationalistic focus. Black prison gangs were born out of a struggle for civil treatment despite being incarcerated. The number one black prison gang is former Black Panther, George Jackson's Black Guerrilla Family, organized in 1966 out of San Quentin (Leet, Rush, and Smith, 1997). The Melanics organized in Michigan's Jackson Prison in 1982 became an immediate threat to the Michigan's Department of Corrections (Knox, 2004(d)). Clarence 13X's Five Percent Nation (predominantly found in New York and New Jersey), appeared on the scene and even though the Five Percenters rebuke the gang label in lieu of mastering numerical science to achieve God status, their illegal conduct has become serious cause for concern (Corbiscello, 2004; Leet, Rush, and Smith, 1997).

Black gangsterism evolved from black activism and yet the entire historical record will reveal that the founders of these street gangs played an integral part in the transformation of gangs into dead end organizations. Masculinity is negotiated in socially disorganized ghettos that have become black colonies dominated by gangsterism. This type of environment represents a gangland, an environment where behavior is governed by codes that dictate how respectable masculinity is seized and maintained. In an environment where deprivation dominates, gangsterism is the standard lifestyle and the seriousness of becoming a respected gang banger has led to fatal consequences. (Cureton, 2002; Anderson, 1999).

THE EMERGENT GANGSTERISM PERSPECTIVE: MANHOOD IS AS ESSENTIAL AS THE AIR I BREATHE

Mainstream society and community macro and micro structural, cultural, and social conditions have led to the birth of collective black activism and black gangsterism. Predominantly, black male community activist groups were born out of defiance and resistance to systemic political and social agendas that denied black personhood. However, the failures and/or shortcomings of collective black activism paved the way for black gangsterism (a culture that promotes manhood as its omnipotent form of social power and one that dictates survival of the fittest in a resource strained, urban setting). Black gangs were parasitically attached to the lives of residents in economically deprived, resource strained, socially disorganized neighborhoods in the majority of America's cities. The Emergent Gangsterism Perspective (EGP) contends that the black experience involves efforts to survive as human beings in an American democracy with political, economic, social, and less than ideal cultural designs for its black population. More specifically, the social organization of gangsterism appears to be a manifestation of a destructive social structure that seemed to wage an intensive campaign that both challenged and denied black manhood through four community transitional stages: defined community (stage 1: 1920-1929); community conversion (stage 2: 1930-1965), gangster colonization (stage 3: 1966-1989); and gangster politicalization (stage 4:1990 well into the 21st century). The theme that seems to rise to the surface when examining the voices of intellectuals, culturalists, ethnographers, religious leaders and notable experienced gangsters, appears to be that becoming a block hustler or gangster is empowering for males looking to achieve some measure of social success in spite of residential limitations.

During the defined community stage (1920-1929), blacks with employable abilities, skills and talents relocated to municipalities that seemed to provide the best opportunity to fully participate in America's money market system. The mass migration of southern blacks seeking better employment opportunities and social conditions landed many of them in northeastern and northwestern locales. The competition class of whites (those with equally employable skills) became consumed by social panic related to the potential of having their economic livelihood threatened and social lifestyles intruded upon. Whites' responses to blacks' presence were community covenants, discrimination, inter-racial predation and all other social mannerisms indicative of racial displeasure. The result was a creation of structural (neighborhood), cultural (norms governing civil behavior), and social (access to public areas of leisure) barriers, which segregated blacks' into what became black colonies. By virtue of social isolation and segregation, blacks' found themselves residents of an independent colony, a viable, racially homogenous community where people became intimately connected by a shared legacy, culture, experience, and value system.

Residents of these black communities seemed focused on collective morality, and universal well being through encouraging healthy family dynamics and positive social networks. Moreover, there seemed to be a high value placed on cultural and spiritual growth, while providing concrete examples of how to secure resources, and opportunities for the benefit of improving life chances (Nisbet, 1966; Frazier, 1957). Perhaps for reasons of public jealousy and feelings of social threat, black communities remained the target of injustice, oppression, and hate crimes from local and state institutions that seemed to protect the employment and social network interests of the white competition class. Blacks simply would not submit nor resign themselves to prohibitions relative to their human existentialism or constitutional infringements; thus, local pushes for civil equalities in employment, housing, education, and freedom of choice relative to public accommodation as well as demands for non-discretionary law enforcement fueled a nationwide civil rights movement. Ultimately, civil rights affordances at the local, state and federal levels opened the doors of opportunity whereby blacks who were educated, professionally trained, experienced, and apprenticed were positioned to successfully integrate or become functional members in mainstream society. Intra-racial social change had arrived in the form of black flight. One of the more damaging aspect of black flight for the black underclass was cultural (includes mental and spiritual) separation because the economic, cultural and social gap between the black middle and underclass widened and the black underclass' functional connection with mainstream society was lost (West, 2002; Anderson, 1999; Short 1997; Dyson, 1996; Wilson 1996; Wilson, 1987; 1973; and Frazier, 1957).

During the community conversion stage (1930-1965), the black community suffered structural, economic, social and cultural declination because of economic distress associated with the Great Depression (1930-early1940's) and resource drain due to intra-racial distancing associated with the civil rights movement (1955-1965) (McCorkle and Miethe 2002; Marable, 1998; Ashmore, 1997; Wilson, 1996; Shaw and McKay, 1942). A significant proportion of unskilled blacks simply were not equipped with the appropriate tools, talents, and shills to take advantage of the numerous opportunities to improve their life chances, which produced urban poor black enclaves.

Federal, state, and local financial aid, and resource assistance was reduced to an insignificant contribution, which created a community freeze in terms of functional citizenship sustainability (Short, 1997; Wilson, 1996; Wilson; 1987). With little to no resources trickling into these black unsettled neighborhoods, black families spiraled into dysfunction with adult males turning to alternative illegitimate means to secure resources and money, and disgruntled youth (fed up with witnessing their parents' cyclical failure and suffering) created a counter-culture where masculinity was tempered by frustration and aggression (Cureton, 2008; Agnew 2006; Anderson, 1999; McCall 1995; Hutchinson, 1998; Wilson, 2002; and Katz, 1988).

As jobs disappeared so did the working class father. The neighborhoods began seeing more and more street corner social networks that tuned into criminogenic opportunities to secure a lifestyle more individualistic than family oriented. Hustlers, pimps, drug pushers, common street thugs and petty criminals dominated the neighborhood streets and as conventional pursuits and morality faded, street ethics emerged. A social milieu indicative of physical prowess, troublesome reputations, and depravity became codes of conduct (Anderson, 1999; and Miller, 1958).

Anderson states

> At the heart of the code is the issue of respect-loosely defined as being treated right or being granted one's props (or proper due) or the deference one deserves. However, in the troublesome public environment of the inner city as people increasingly feel buffeted by forces beyond their control, what one deserves in the way of respect becomes ever more problematic and uncertain. This situation in turn further opens up the issue of respect to sometimes intense interpersonal negotiation, at times resulting in altercations. In the street culture, especially among young people, respect is viewed as almost an external entity, one that is hard-won but easily lost—and so must constantly be guarded. The rules of the code in fact provide a framework for negotiating respect. With the right amount of respect, individuals can avoid being bothered in public. This security is important, for if they are bothered, not only may they face physical danger, but they will have been disgraced or dissed (disrespected)....The hard reality of the world of the street can be traced to the profound sense of alienation from mainstream society and its institutions felt by many poor inner-city black people, particularly the young. The code of the street is actually a cultural adaptation to a profound lack of faith in the police and the judicial system (Anderson, 1999:33-34).

In many respects the code of the street became normative expectations governing interpersonal behavior when confronted by personal challenges. The potential for violence intensifies conflict resolution forcing trivial matters to often escalate to more serious feuds as combatants often over anticipate one another's conflict resolution style. The scarcity of resources and materials increases the value of reputation because reputation becomes social currency that yields the kind of fear and respect that is important for survival in urban depressed neighborhoods. Those black adult males who became fully immersed into subcultural illegitimacy turned their backs on their family responsibility because the criminogenic lifestyle required more street time and alternatively less family time. The quality of the black family suffered as fathers routinely engaged in deviance, crime and violence, which became dead end realities linked to incarceration and death. Adult black males began disappearing from homes and the streets, which gave way to female headed households with younger males who were catapulted into adult responsibilities.

Fields contends that a damaged relationship between mother and son is a fundamental betrayal because the mother is the son's first love. In instances where this relationship borders on abuse, the son emerges with an attitude reflective of deep disappointment and shame. At some point he will take a stand against the physical abuse but the emotional abuse may be ten times worse, doing far more damage to his manly character. Thus, his pursuit is all about exaggerated manhood. Moreover, too much abuse coming from the mother can take the form of a syndrome that carries consequences for young male dealing with other women, and males identified as the enemy probably don't stand a chance against young males who are consumed with rage (Fields, 2008). Therefore in the most basic way, the most important institution to fail young black males was the family (Anderson, 1999; Anderson 1990).

Young black males in economic and socially depressed areas, with families that defaulted on its ability to be a functional socialization agent experienced wholesale disappointment, confusion and exposure to dreadful conditions. These bitter black youth sought out like circumstanced individuals and formed subcultures or juvenocracies that emphasized respect, material acquisition, money, sexual exploits and street prestige. These young boys went after the same indicators of manhood that they witnessed their adult male role models on the block pursue. Essentially, juvenocracies or subcultures of enraged young males participated in deviance, crime, and violence to seize some measure of economic, resource, material, and social success, and the major reason for fully embracing juvenocracies was because it represented an opportunity to overcome macro and micro level failures of American institutions (i.e. local and state government assistance programs, businesses, schools, police departments, and the family) (Cureton, 2009; Hilliard, Zimmerman, and Zimmerman, 2006; and Dyson, 1996).

El-Hajj Malik El-Shabazz (Malcolm X) contends

And because I had been a hustler, I knew better than all whites knew. And better than nearly all of the black leaders knew, that actually the most dangerous black man in America was the ghetto hustler. Why do I say this? The hustler, out there in the ghetto jungles, has less respect for the white power structure than any other Negro in North America. The ghetto hustler is internally restrained by nothing. He has no religion, no concept of morality, no civic responsibility, no fear-nothing. To survive, he is out there constantly preying upon others, probing for any human weakness like a ferret. The ghetto hustler is forever frustrated, restless, and anxious for some action. Whatever he undertakes, he commits himself to it fully, absolutely. What makes the ghetto hustler yet more dangerous is his glamour image to the school-dropout youth in the ghetto. These ghetto teenagers see the hell caught by their parents struggling to get somewhere, or see that they have given up struggling in the prejudiced, intolerant white man's world.

The ghetto teenagers make up their minds they would rather be like the hustlers whom they see dressed sharp and flashing money and displaying no respect for anybody or anything. So the ghetto youth become attracted to the hustler worlds of dope, thievery, prostitution, and general crime and immorality. It scared me the first time I really saw the danger of these ghetto teenagers if they are ever sparked to violence (El-Hajj Malik El-Shabazz 1964:340).

A precursor to subscribing to the negative aspects (crippling violence, residency in penal colonies, and fatal victimization) of street code ethics and juvenocracies is the realization that the American Dream is not attainable. Unfortunately, the shady side of the Civil Rights Movement was its inability to secure better life chances for every black American. Civil rights shortcomings (failure to force the doors of opportunism open wide enough to be inclusive) and black flight (intra-racial abandonment) functioned to create double marginalization and ultimately a permanent underclass (Wilson, 1996; Wilson, 1987).

Gangster colonization (stage three 1966-1989) was a period when street gangs became the number one socialization agent for males searching for an identity in a gangland. The side-effect of community conversion was social misery (a seed of discontent for street gangs in hood enclaves). Hood enclaves represent segmented groups of territorial male gangs who have become bitterly divided as a result of structural, social, and cultural deprivation. These self-ordained street kings represent the strongest force in the neighborhood. The gang dictates residential activity and assumes ownership of youths' psychological strength, identity, social development, perspective, socialization, and culture (Cureton, 2008; Williams 2004; Shakur, 1993; and Skogan, 1990). Most suburban Americans understand the meaning of the bad side of town (chocolate city places or areas with high concentrations of underclass blacks); and thus, have no social interest in the predominantly black areas of Southeast District of Columbia, Philadelphia, New Jersey, New York, Chicago, Florida, Seattle and South Central, Los Angeles. When these places become dominated by gangs they essentially transform into environments where young black males are brutally baptized by experiences with crime and violence; and therefore, find themselves making gangster choices with long standing gangster consequences. Chicago and South Central have been ground zero for traditional street gangs and South Central is still referred to as the gang capital of America.

Stanley "Tookie" Williams, co founder of the Crips stated, "As I grew older, I realized that it wasn't the typical urban ghetto-it had a deceptive look of prosperity. It was a west side colony of poverty behind a façade of manicured lawns and clean streets, of Cadillacs, Fords, and Chevys. The neighborhood was a shiny red apple rotting away at the core" (Williams, 2004:10).

Mad Dog (74 Hoover Gangster from South Central) states, "the condition of the hood is wounded…All kinda ways, financially, mental. It's wounded, it's hurt, it's poverty, it's envy, it's death. That's what is happening in the neighborhood right now! No nothing. The hood is draining, draining the life out of you. The hood is missing a lot of strength, so people are going to do whatever they got to do to survive. If that means gang banging, then there it is" (Cureton, 2008:22).

Duck (112 Hoover Gangster from South Central): "I look at South Central as a community of poverty. Some neighborhoods don't have recreational parks for kids, so what are kids to do?" (Cureton, 2008:29).

Intra-racial abandonment and sentiments of black elitism (underclass blacks are not deserving of functional opportunities), strained resources, community crowding, physical and social deprivation, black-on-black criminal and murderous victimization eventually led to urban unrest in many cities with high concentrations of urban poor blacks (Sloan 2007; West 2001; Alonso 1999; Dyson 1996; and Geschwender, 1971). Constantly confronting the dreadful realities of urban structural and social declination and immediate suppression and oppression weighs heavily on black males.

Stanley "Tookie" Williams: "As a beneficiary of more than five hundred years of slavery, I was left only scattered remnants of a broke culture. Exposed to a multitude of ambiguous mostly negative influences, I would pass through my young life with cultural neglect and a profound identity crisis. Though I knew I was black. I had no real perspective on being black. I had absorbed the common negative black stereotypes that eventually made me despise blackness" (Williams, 2004:15).

Stanley "Tookie" Williams offers a personal assessment of self-hate, which infects the social development of urban underclass black youth across the country. According to West (2001), the core of the problem for the urban black underclass is nihilism, a condition likened unto a debilitating disease that arrests the soul, and effectively drains the desire to live. For West, nihilism results from coping with a life of "horrifying meaninglessness, hopelessness, and lovelessness" (West, 2001:22-23).

West states:

> the frightening result is a numbing detachment from others, a self destructive disposition. Life without meaning, hope, and love breeds a coldhearted, mean-spirited outlook that destroys both the individual and others (West, 2001:22-23).
> . . . Nihilism represents a condition of the soul (much like a disease) that requires routine doses of success, earned respect, personal accountability, a love ethic (self-love and love for others), meaningful identity formations and sense of purpose (affirms self-worth); for without these approaches, nihilism is a condition that can re-occur (West, 2001:29).

The macro level offense against blacks was that opportunities for functional citizenship seemingly did not extend to include the black underclass. Another macro level offense was intra-racial segregation, isolation, and a sense of captivity within the walls of a nefarious environment. At the micro level, the family simply failed to instill positive self-esteem, and pride that kept young males from feeling alienated and hostile. Perhaps the most damaging family dynamic was the disappearance of the father and/or functional in-home male role models. Voluntarily absent fathers left the duties of raising children to women who became overwhelmed by the prospects of trying to sustain a functional household while raising children. These single mothers for the most part did the best that they could; however, far too many female single headed households became a house of psychological and physical abuse as mothers often took out their stresses and frustration on their children. Specifically, where mothers failed to control their bitterness toward fathers, sons were exposed to excessive messages emphasizing his father's worthlessness. Young boys who fail to recognize that the true source of his mother's bitterness rests with his father and not with him become irritated and perhaps ashamed (Fields, 2008; Agnew, 2006; Gottfredson and Hirschi, 1990; and Simons, Simmons and Wallace, 2004).

Stanley "Tookie" Williams:

> My mother adhered religiously to the Judeo-Christian Bible, in particular Proverb 13:24: He who spareth his rod hateth his son. But he that loveth him chastiseth him betimes (whips him quickly). Yes, my mother loved me deeply, and I regularly felt her love's sting. But compared to the beatings some of my friends received from their parents, I got off easy....Mass incarceration has become a divisive force that splits families and foments a son's resentment for his father. As a youth I often felt emptiness in my life, and not simply for lack of a father's presence. My biological father was a sad example of fatherhood. I yearned for an esteemed black male figure who projected a dynamic image I could strive to emulate or surpass. In different circumstances my chances for success would have increased considerably (Williams, 2004: 4 and 319).

Duck (112 Hoover Gangster from South Central):

yes having a father or positive role model is important because in some cases, I wouldn't never had to pay the dues that I paid or been incarcerated. I wish back then, I would have had a male figure that would have whipped my ass or not so much whip my ass, but show some quality time. Show me another direction, but see I had to get out there, and establish all this for myself. That's why I'm proud to say that four days of the week, I'm a greedy motherfucker. What's mine is mine. I credit myself for who I became. I credit myself for my success and failures (Cureton, 2008:29).

Tookie and Duck's responses underscore the importance of a functional relationship with the mother and the father. The breakup of the family (either by fathers turning away from husbandry and family responsibilities or by fathers going to prison for extended periods of time) creates a void and reasonable doubt concerning the nature of masculinity. The reality is simple, regardless of the reasons(s) families become dysfunctional failure of one or both parents infuses young boys with a sense of urgency to become men, which alternatively seems to set them on a destructive gangster oriented path. The gang then becomes a supporting vessel for black males' addiction to the pursuit of hyper-masculinity that is gained from mastering predatory violence. While the dangerous pursuit of masculine achievements through gangsterism wrecked many black neighborhoods, the destruction never breached the collective conscious of mainstream America until urban unrest became center stage in media coverage. Hood enclave riots were essentially ghetto screams, a physical outpouring of frustration for all of America to witness. Riots or hood revolts erupted as ghetto black residents across the country, suffered collective anomic despair because of an un-measurable amount of inter and intra-racial rejection, social and legal injustice, demoralization and anger. These social rebellions increased public fear, intensified police departments' social regulation and control, dominated media outlet headlines, and for the first time, America was directly confronted with the black street gang and the gang's dangerous potential for destruction (Ashmore, 1997; Marable, 1997; Geschwender, 1971; and Oberschall, 1967).

During gangster politicalization (1990 and well into the 21st century) neighborhoods became governed by street gangs or normative expectations relative to lifestyle in a gangland became the primary focal point. The reality for young boys attempting to negotiate masculinity is that they are confronted with an aggressive gangster lifestyle as soon as they are old enough to start engaging in unsupervised activities (typically ages 7 thru 10). During this period, potential young male gang bangers needed to be properly socialized about the importance of strict adherence to norms governing street protocol, the duties of relative gang status (i.e. gang affiliate, gang member, and gang banger), offenses that become declarations of war, value of gang alliances, war-time maneuvering, seizing control of and protecting turf, drug and gun distribution, expectations regarding revenge, recreation, social access to females and spatial mobility.

Children certainly don't automatically gravitate towards gangsterism in ganglands. In some very critical ways they have already been a witness to the harsh realities of the ghetto. Needless to say, being confined to the home and under the mother's control decreases the frequency of contact with older males who are already positioned to assume the duties of surrogate socialization agents. In other words, once the young boy steps outside, he immediately begins a social reconstruction of self based on environmental realities. It does not take long for young boys to become cognizant of the fact that their structural confinement limits their possibilities for social development. Those goals that seem consistent with the American dream, quickly become denounced as a waste of time given such resource and material acquisitions seem to be reserved for members of the outside world (those not residing in the ghetto). It is not that difficult to imagine that an urban black male would become a gangster simply because gangsterism offers the option to become aligned with an elite group that allows members to transcend economic strain, resource restrictions, and social status denials, and in some small way contributes to some type of righteous lifestyle (having respect is equivalent to righteous in the ghetto) (Cureton, 2008; Williams, 2004; Anderson, 1999; and Shakur, 1993).

Foremost, the gang positioned itself as the gateway to respectable manhood. The gang seemingly offered the promise of family acceptance, a bond based on brotherhood, economic and social success, encouragement and support for disciplined violence, and help with the pitfalls associated with living in gang dominated areas. Original gangsters assumed the responsibility of teaching the nuances of gangsterism (i.e. survival, territorial claims, gang set configurations and leadership, color coding, hand signs, verbal ques, decisions for gang warfare, and tactical maneuvering, anatomy of drive-bys, gang alliances, truces, and drug distribution) as well as the rules governing ascending to the ultimate goal of becoming an Original Gangster (O.G.).

Sanyika Shakur (aka Monster Kody) intimated that his socialization into the gangster sub-culture involved three steps toward achieving Original Gangster Status (O.G.): "(1) you must build the reputation of your name/ you as an individual; (2) you must build your name in association with your particular set, so that when your name is spoken your set is also spoken of in the same breath, for it is synonymous; and (3) you must establish yourself as a promoter of Crip or Blood, depending, of course, on which side of the color bar you live" (Shakur, 1993:15). Kody adopted Monster as his gang name after the police commented on the disfiguring assault of a victim that Kody had stomped for twenty minutes. The police said "that the person responsible for this was a monster" (Shakur, 1993: 13).

Stanley "Tookie" Williams certainly participated in actions that made him a Superior Crip: "as a Crip I could strive to be legendary. It was my intent to make Crip and Tookie synonymous, a matched set and a terrorizing force among every other black gang in South Central....I seized every angle in life to define myself as being somebody. It didn't matter how ruthless or despicable I had to become in the realm of ganghood as long as I was the best" (Williams, 2004: 106 and 184).

Duck's (112 Hoover Gangster from South Central) entire gang banging history represented a personal endeavor to become a black Caesar:

Let me give you some insight. I fought for my life. I fought for a living. This just didn't start today. I knew my options were to stay a winner, and not become a loser, and have a audience that's gonna laugh, and pass on the word that he ain't nothing because I am something...Me, myself, through my career of being incarcerated, I done had the pleasure of meeting ghetto superstars from all walks of fame. They didn't fuck me, and I didn't fuck them. We respected one another, whether it came to pushing, and shoving or knuckling up. A understanding was brought about. I'm Duck and you are you. A motherfucker didn't want to fight tomorrow, so there was a understanding. Unfortunately, gangsterism lives throughout and within me, mentally and physically. Remember I told you that I was challenged by a brother, and I brought harm to him. I stabbed him up and kicked him around. I had some assistance that thought it was of some fun. We kept it real, and took a deal because we was busted without a doubt. Here it is we already in prison, we gonna create and continue to commit crimes. I don't regret doing what I had to do because that added to my reputation of being a down young brother. I never really had problems and I can't recall motherfuckers coming up to me, and fucking me up. Hey, I'm a do or die motherfucker, and if you ain't gonna kill me, don't fuck with me (Cureton, 2008:33).

It could be that the most significant component for gangster politicalization is to settle on the realities of a God spirit. Submission to the doctrine of a God Spirit could lead to acts of peace and civility as resolutions to otherwise fatal conflicts. However, coming to grips with the imagined reality that a God Spirit has no control, forces young males to assume a God complex, which directly contributes to predatory street politicking (aggressive pursuit of respectable manhood). Gangsterism may be fuelled by individuals (who have experienced what appears to be Godless realities) relegating a God Spirit to a chance encounter in the afterlife. Through consistent trials and tribulations, and enduring the finality of comrades' mortality, the perception that individuals would benefit by living according to God is supplanted by personal assessments that God is irrelevant (Cureton, 2008; Williams, 2004; and Shakur, 1993).

Sanyika Shakur (aka Monster):

> Retribution is a natural reaction. It's easy to persuade the general public of your righteousness when you control major media. But those of us who control nothing are in the precarious position of having someone guess what our position is. This leaves quite a large gap for misinformation. Who fired the first shot? Who knows?! But, too, who cares, when one of theirs is lying in a pool of blood with his brains blown out. This question becomes weightless in the aftermath of a shooting where someone had died. Thus the goal becomes the elimination of the shooter or as many of his comrades as possible. This inevitably leads to war-a full-scale mobilization of as many troops as needed to achieve the desired effect: funerals. (Shakur, 1993:57)…My thing was this: I didn't believe there was a God. I just had no faith in what I couldn't see, feel, taste or smell. All my life I have seen the power of life and death in the hands of men and boys. If I shot at someone and I hit him and he died, who took his life? Me or God? Was it predestined that on this day at this time I would specifically push this guy out of existence? I never believed that. I believed that I hunted him, caught him, and killed him. I had lived in too much disorder to believe that there was an actual design to this world. So I had a problem with believing in anything other than myself" (Shakur, 1993: 227).

My encounters with South Central gangsters and relative immersion (through field research) in Crip and Blood neighborhoods, certainly leads me to conclude (and I realize the subjective nature of making such a statement) that the gangster sub-culture seems beholden to a negative energy that has manipulated gang banging residents to incorporate fatal predation as an automatic default mechanism for social challenges, misunderstandings, and conflicts (Cureton, 2008).

LOOKING THROUGH THE REAR VIEW MIRROR

Stanley "Tookie" Williams, cofounder of the infamous Crip gang, suggested that his youthful experiences should be inclusive of the impact of colonialism relative to the social development of black lower class urban males. Stanley "Tookie" Williams appears to be suggesting that external race legacy produced dysfunction and created a devastating volatile sub-culture.

Stanley "Tookie" Williams:

> The problem, I now believe, was the absence of a valid psychoanalytic model designed to address black people, the black experience…My mother might have

fared better standing me before some of the street-corner winos. It was rumored that a few of them graduated summa cum laude. Some of their alcoholic rants and prophetic warnings were more learned than the lectures of many academics. At least their analyses of racism, slavery, poverty, police brutality, politics, child psychology, and other topics were gained based on grassroots experience. (Williams; 2007:45-46).

The Emergent Gangsterism Perspective (EGP) (though originally concentrating on the social conversion of South Central, Los Angeles' communities) perhaps has some explanatory value for black hood enclaves characterized by subordination and powerlessness, opportunity channeling, resource strain, psychological rejection, substandard quality of life, institutional mass incarceration, marginalization, isolation and alienation, and intra-racial victimization. Arguably these conditions ultimately became seeds of discontent from which a rebellious harvest featuring Crips (i.e. Rollin 20's through 60's, Hoover, Eight Tray Gangsters, Grape Street, East and West Side, Avalon Garden, Shot Gun, Kitchen, Compton, Venice, etc.,) and Bloods (i.e. Athens, Brims, Bishops, Bounty Hunters, Denver Lanes, Pirus, and Swans) out of South Central, Los Angeles and Chicago's three major street gangs Devil's Disciples, P-Stones, and Vice Lords (Cureton, 2009; Sloan, 2007; Knox and Papachristos, 2002; Alonso 1999, and Dawley 1992). Moreover, there are so many more socially disorganized areas with severe structural, economic, social and cultural deprivation in this country that there is certain to be street corner groups, cliques, posses, crews, and street elites that have become primary in black males' social development. Therefore, future research is needed to examine the social realities of the ghetto that seem consistent with the community social changes discussed by the Emergent Gangsterism Perspective. Certainly, offering the intellectual contributions of El-Hajj Malik El-Shabazz (Malcolm X), Elijah Anderson, Cornel West, Michael Dyson, Eldridge Cleaver, Thomas Merton, Ruth Benedict, and Sterling Tucker as well as notable gangsters, Stanley "Tookie" Williams, and Sanyika Shakur, and Hoovers (Duck and Mad Dog) only validates the importance of researching race legacy and gangland realities as these could be significantly related to the lifestyle choices of the (estimated) 2.2 million black adult prisoner and juvenile detainees in America.

While in prison Cleaver offered that whenever, he felt himself gravitating towards becoming relaxed, sentimental or too weak to combat the harsh mandates of prison, he would ponder Thomas Merton's (1948) description of Harlem (in the book The Seven Storey Mountain). Cleaver ponders:

here in this huge, dark, steaming slum, hundreds of thousands of Negroes are herded together like cattle, most of them with nothing to eat and nothing to do.

All the senses and imagination and sensibilities and emotions and sorrows and desires and hopes and ideas of a race with vivid feelings and deep emotional reactions are forced in upon themselves, bound inward by an iron ring of frustration: the prejudice that hems them in with its four insurmountable walls. In this huge cauldron, inestimable natural gifts, wisdom, love, music, science, poetry, are stamped down and left to boil with the dregs of an elementally corrupted nature, and thousands upon thousands of souls are destroyed by vice and misery and degradation, obliterated, wiped out, washed from the register of the living, dehumanized. What has not been devoured, in your dark furnace, Harlem, by marijuana, by gin, by insanity, hysteria, syphilis? (Cleaver, 1968:55).

If reading this passage forces a man to become desensitized or prison hardened, what should we conclude about the social negotiations of black residents in urban cities just like Harlem, Chicago or South Central, Los Angeles? At best the black experience in America represents a racial legacy of progression in spite of critical assaults on human dignity and at worse this experience, when investing in a critical analysis of the ghetto, remains an African-American life course tragedy.

Chapter Four

Gangs by Any Other Name

Omega Fraternalism and Hoover Gangsterism

I am fully aware of the consequences that may come from offering this information for public consumption and I enthusiastically embrace whatever may come. The main purpose of this chapter is to demonstrate that black masculinity is contextually specific to environment. That being said being a college student (while making black males slightly better off in terms of potential for assimilation) does not mean that these men are better than urban poor black males (who openly affiliate with whatever group that is perceived as critical to successful manhood). Somehow integration and/or successful matriculation into socially legitimate institutions has created a middle class of blacks who seem to collectively frown upon the permanent underclass and the result is that class transcending universal brotherhood is virtually non-existent.

I am a member of the Omega Psi Phi Fraternity and have been since 1991. I became an underground affiliate with the organization on August 3rd 1991, while a student at Washington State University, in Pullman Washington. My signature individual name is Solodog and my signature line name is No Retreat-No Surrender. My formal initiation into the organization was completed on November 22nd 1991 through Chi Alpha Alpha, an intermediate chapter out of Spokane, Washington. Why are these dates different? It's the difference between being "made or pledging" and also navigating through the protocol endorsed by International Headquarters through the fraternity's mandated Intake Program. My reward for pledging, I became a Que-Dog, with chapter credibility and the entitlements to travel and not be harassed because of the knowledge and style that could only be ascertained through pledging. My reward for going through the Intake Program, I became an official card carrying member of Omega Psi Phi, with all rights and privileges. Omega Psi Phi Fraternity took an official stance against hazing in the 1950's and officially banned pledging and any form of hazing in 1989/1990, yet the culture thrives in so many bastardized forms that the fraternity is sprinkled with renegades (college men who have been pledged and are Ques through unsupervised underground programs, but have never been formally initiated into the fraternity). It's a subcultural crisis that has plagued Omega Psi Phi since 1990. Omega Psi Phi does not recognize any brother that has not been formally initiated, but the undergraduate Que-Dog culture is split, the majority of brothers don't recognize renegades, while others are more concerned with "how you were made."

Even the best efforts to clean up this practice (mandated certifications for intake procedures, tweaking the official intake process to somewhat satisfy the desire to "get to know a brother and make him prove his loyalty and/or desire to be an Omega, fraternity protocol relative to polygraph tests, chapter insurance liability requirements, fraternity sanctions, legal sanctions, criminal consequences, and school related expulsions), fail to deter some version of a pledge process because there will always be young men, who seek to align themselves with an organization that provides instant reputational social currency. In other words, there could have never been a Que-Dog pledge sub-culture, (a bastardized program derived from the unique Lampados Club) attached to the Omega Psi Phi Fraternity, without willing participants. Honestly, the Omega Psi Phi Fraternity Incorporated is an organization of predominantly African-American college and graduate men who share a mindset to be a beacon of morality, civility, intelligence, task completion, leadership and service to universities and communities in all recognized American states and International locals, yet there is a subculture in the organization's blood stream that satisfies the urge to be "the bad boys." Thus, Omega Psi Phi has an official membership that will never let go of the Que-Dog image (even though there is an intra-fraternal movement to distance Omega Psi Phi from any canine reference) and an un-official cast of renegade characters that "got made" but never became officially recognized.

WHAT CHAPTER YOU CLAIMING BROTHER?
WHAT HOOD YOU CLAIMING HOMIE?

On November 17, 1911, the Omega Psi Phi Fraternity was founded at Howard University (by three undergraduates: Edgar A. Love, Oscar J. Cooper, and Frank Coleman–with the advisor being Dr. Ernest E. Just) for African-American college men who had demonstrated a certain level of academic excellence and community service. Omega's fundamental principles (manhood, scholarship, perseverance, and uplift), belief in God, perspectives on religion, friendship, love, and respect for family and community provide the foundation for an ethical standard of living that both graduate and undergraduate members obligate themselves to live by. Omega Psi Phi is a fraternal brotherhood of future professional men (undergraduates) and graduated professional men (e.g. bishops, ministers, and preachers, medical and social scientists, entrepreneurs, corporate owners, business executives, politicians, lawyers, judges, civil rights leaders, orators, soldiers, academic and literary scholars, entertainers, musicians, athletes, and artists) (Gill, 1963; Dreer, 1940).

However, one of the fraternity's unacknowledged burdens is its indirect link to urban street gangs. Without question, black fraternities were not founded for the purpose of recruiting gang affiliated college men and the fraternity has a policy that prohibits membership for those individuals who have criminal records. Apparently, some potential undergraduate candidates for membership into Omega Psi Phi do an excellent job at hiding their level of gang affiliation, which is difficult to assess (legally and professionally). Undergraduate candidates are recruited because they have established themselves enough to meet the rather strict requirements for membership (sophomore status at a four year institution, with a minimum cumulative grade point average of 2.5 or better on a 4.0 grading scale). Fraternity chapters are unaware of their candidates' social circumstances prior to college, which can include various levels of gang banging activity or simple affiliation by virtue of living in a gangland. Whatever the case, the fraternity has a small but significant numbers of undergraduate members who are also affiliated with gangs. Undergraduate chapters most likely to have gang affiliated undergraduate members or members who at some point participated in collective "thugism" (street subculture--collective group deviance/crime and violence) prior to college, would be those university recognized chapters located in areas where gangs are prevalent (e.g. Washington, Oregon, California, Arizona, Missouri, Colorado, Utah, Illinois, Kansas City, New York, Philadelphia, Texas, Florida, Alabama, Nebraska, Arkansas, Louisiana, North and South Carolina). I implore you to be cautious and not rush to make grand sweeping indictments about Omega Psi Phi as a haven for gang affiliates because Omega Psi Phi has a significantly higher percentage of proven black men who have traditionally made and continue to contribute positive, functional, and life sustaining tangible and intangible services to American society. Nevertheless, Omega's link to gang members should not be surprising and is definitely not a unique (in the sense that this is only indicative of Omega) phenomenon given that African-American fraternities and African-American gangs are similar in many ways. Despite having different social backgrounds, males seem to gravitate towards those social networks deemed relevant for success. This is not to suggest that every man needs fraternities or gangs but it does imply that males use some type of group to successfully navigate social realities specific to campus and street environments.

My mentor, Charles Tittle once told me (back in 1993) that I would not be able to make a living doing gang research. I took his word on that for some time but the subject just kept creeping into my life in ways that I am still coming to grips with now. The black gang phenomenon has held center court in my academic career through field research, publishing, teaching, professional service and community outreach.

Perhaps it is because I appreciate black masculinity and the desire to survive whatever the circumstances. It's hard being a black man in America because while legitimate opportunities are possible and potentially forthcoming, the social, economic, structural, and cultural, trappings are seemingly infinite. My historical diary reveals that I am from the ghetto, the projects, from fatherlessness, and a mother who spent my formative years in and out of prison and/or running from warrants, yet I survived to become the person I am today. Still no matter the doom and gloom "black male statistics" that I obviously did not fall victim to, I am no different from the ghetto hustler/ black gangster. While it is true that I have earned my blessed condition, I still share the same racial ascription as black gangsters and I acknowledge that in any instance where I am better off (economically, educationally, socially, housing, life, leisure, social comforts and convenience) that does not make me (in no way, shape, form or fashion) better than another black man. Fully acknowledging this idea removes barriers of separation and permits embracing universal brotherhood. I am pleased to have the kind of mentor that I can share these thoughts with and he (being a white male) is receptive, encouraging and direct enough to advise me to work to create an academic fingerprint (make a sociological contribution) that reflects my ideas about race and masculinity. Dr. Tittle's voice rings in my head "well Steve, what are you going to do about it, are you going to simply talk about it or give it the sociological attention it deserves?"

The court of public opinion (heavily influenced by media, politics, legal agents and victimization accounts) and even mainstream criminologists seems to embrace the common theme that black gangsterism is a pathological mode of operation that started in the early 1970's and coincides with the so-called underground, black market economy of illegal vices. Before offering this as social facts about black gangsterism, a thorough historical investigation is warranted. I am interested in black gangsterism because black street gangs deserve the courtesy of some type of generational presentation (inclusive of every social, economic, structural and cultural ingredient) and legacy revelation (experienced and expressed) by gangsters. Certainly, black gangsterism has been offered up for public consumption through academic scholarship, criminal justice-related policies, and infamously portrayed in Hollywood but these areas have questionable authenticity, are not free from prejudice, racial ignorance and politics, marketing and maybe welded to traditional fears about black men and simply fail the test of having an intra-racial perspective (Cureton, 2008).

Some of Hoover's Original Gangster from Five Deuce, Seven Four, and Eleven Deuce have said that "you would not understand the hood, if you ain't never been to the hood so if you want to know why we do what we do, just bring your ass down to South Central Los Angeles." This statement challenges us to go directly to the environment for understanding of black gang culture. It also seems to foster mutual alienation and does nothing to indicate who would be welcome. However, after experiencing Hoover first hand, I completely understand the statement to be consistent with South Central's economic poverty and social deprivation because these conditions significantly impact their choices and behaviors. My knowledge of the Hoover Gang (formerly known as Hoover Groovers, Hoover Crips, and the contemporary version of new generation Hoovers prefer Hoover Criminals) is based on field research dating back to 1999 (when I first step foot on Hoover turf). Since then I have consistently revisited Hoover, meeting and fellowshipping with Original Gangsters and new generation Hoovers. Hoover consists of nine branches (covering 43rd to 52nd, to 59th, to 74th, to 83rd, to 92nd, to 94th, to 107th, to112th) (Cureton, 2008:7). Although some of these branches have been inactive for a number of years, Hoovers (Groovers, Crips, or Criminals depending on which generation you talk to) remains the third largest black street gang in South Central, Los Angeles. Even though times have changed and California adopted a name change for South Central to South, Los Angeles (on April 9th, 2003), the conditions that perpetuate black gangsterism have not diminished at all; therefore, South Los Angeles is still very much South, Central Los Angeles, in that it remains a gangland (Cureton, 2008:1).

The attraction to Hoover and gangs for that matter depends on males' outlook relative to their future. Unfortunately, social, economic, cultural, and spiritual deprivation have altered black young males' perceptions concerning their realistic conventional life chances. Residency on Hoover and perhaps other similarly circumstanced socially disorganized environments forces males to restrict their realities to the immediacy of ghetto. If the core ingredients of the ghetto reflect, poverty, street level challenges to masculinity, a black market economy with genuine employment opportunities and groups that control turf and opportunity for some type of successful lifestyle, then masculine pursuits will gravitate towards those ingredients. Far too many of Hoover's young resident males become inspired by the perceived benefits (i.e. money, social status and prestige, power, respect, and sense of belonging to something that matters) related to gangsterism and don't subscribe to conventional words of wisdom warning them stay away from the detrimental realities of a gangster's

lifestyle. Gangs are supporting vessels for gang bangers' addiction to the superior reputation that is gained from mastering predatory violence.

Moreover, the accessibility of the Hoover gang is an attractive alternative
for vulnerable, young boys who don't have contributing fathers and/or positive male role models. Hoover's appeal is strengthened as it becomes a vital
substitute for black boys who at least acknowledge that the gang is an important group and may in fact be a mandatory choice for young boys in pursuit
of manhood in a gangland. Gangsterism has generational continuity because
being a gang member and having a direct relationship with an entity as powerful as the gang (in a gangland) transcends race and other social restrictions
related to poverty. Once an individual pledges allegiance to a gang and fully
invests in gangster activities, the chances of a complete break from the gang
is the same as his chances of being born black and waking up white.

Comparing a fraternity of college educated men with gangs that may
have a cast of questionable characters will not sit well with any one of the
five nationally known and highly esteemed historically black fraternities
(Omega Psi Phi, Kappa Alpha Psi, Alpha Phi Alpha, Phi Beta Sigma and
Iota Phi Theta). After all, our fraternities are supposed to represent a level
of civility and intelligence far more advanced than those un-educated, unskilled and morally deprived gangs residing in urban poor areas. Fraternal
criticisms may continue along the lines of accusing me of disrespecting the
tradition of black fraternities. My response to this criticism is that there is
no disrespect intended; rather, I am simply examining a reality that should
not continue to be ignored for the sake of superficial appearances. Before
further delusional criticisms are offered, I'd caution pondering those unspo-
ken behaviors that our beloved fraternities continue to participate in, which
are very much indicative of street gangsterism. I am no stranger to that hard
but fair road into the Omega Psi Phi Fraternity and I know the implications
of it well enough to give an experienced voice to it. What's more we need
only turn our attention to the 20th and 21st century where at least four out
of the five fraternities listed have victimized their pledges enough to be
held criminally responsible for assault, faced civil lawsuits and/or have
had underground non-sanctioned pledge processes where young men have
either been seriously injured enough to require medical care or have lost
their lives.

Table 1 lists provisions that males are likely to receive if they elect to join a
black fraternity or street gang. According to Table 1, joining a college fraternity offers 15 out of 20 of the same provisions a male residing in a gangland
would receive by joining a gang. Both black fraternities and street gangs have
origins that date back to the early 1900's. Individuals seeking membership
into these groups are fully aware of the groups' campus or street tradition. In

fact, it is the idea of association with a campus or street respected brotherhood that attracts individuals to these groups. Fundamentally, just as gangs offer opportunities for social success on the streets, African-American fraternities provide channels for success on the college campus.

Additionally, black fraternities offer members an instant reputation boost and provide its members with social status and prestige that is comparable to the social boost in reputation and social status that gang members receive on the streets. Black fraternities (similar to street gangs) are also organized around exclusively unique characteristics in that the fraternity provides bond, love, closeness, loyalty, brotherhood, sense of belonging, protection, symbols, colors, hand signs, rituals, gestures, demeanor, and claims to territories and even people on campus. Black fraternities often compete with one another and this competition has at times escalated to physical confrontations that (except for fatal violence) resemble gang brawls. Whether we are talking about undergraduate college fraternities or street groups, the glaring similarity is that both represent a group of men who are "down" for one another. Any confrontations, particularly physical, with one member usually results in some form of retaliation from those members he goes to for assistance. Brothers who are "down" (for one another) will not hesitate to protect their "frat brothers." Brothers from the same undergraduate chapter share such deep loyalties and exclusive brotherly love that they will meet any opposition with physical resistance when necessary. The union of fraternity members coupled by exclusive brotherly love promotes ideas and actions aimed to "be thy brother's keeper," which is very similar to Hoovers promotion of "lookin' out for the Homie."

The significant differences between gangs and fraternities are that gangs are not socially acceptable (although they use to be during the 1960's period of social activism), gangs don't have educational criteria (university standards) for membership (although gang members are required to know critical information about their gang), and gangs endorse the use of weaponry to settle disputes and thrive off of lethal predation whereas these activities would become justifiable reasons to denounce and in fact eliminate black fraternities on campus. Essentially, the major difference appears to be contextual. Fraternities are organized around the campus setting and gangs are organized according to the realities of the street. For example, Hoover has many "Sets," which are determined by where one lives in a territory covering 43rd to 112th street. Similarly fraternities, given the institutional setting, have chapters, which are as numerous as the universities that officially recognize them. Sometimes Sets will have problems amongst themselves, which are resolved either through talking it out or by violence. No Set can afford to tolerate any level of disrespect, so if situations can be

Table 1. Comparing Features of Omega Psi Phi Fraternity and Hoover Gang

	Omega Psi Phi Fraternity	*Hoover Gang*
Group Provisions	*College Fraternity*	*Traditional Street Gang*
Acceptable institution for affiliation	Yes	No
Family legacy/generational replacement	Yes	Somewhat
Educational criteria for membership	Yes	No
Opportunity to affiliate with a traditional group	Yes	Yes
Connection with respected brotherhood	Yes	Yes
Opportunities for social success	Yes	Yes
Provides reputational boost	Yes	Yes
Behavior governed by subcultural normative expectations	Yes	Yes
Claim territory	Yes	Yes
Provides Protections	Yes	Yes
Participate in deviant/violent group confrontations	Yes	Yes
Philosophy of being down for one another	Yes	Yes
Division based on location	Yes	Yes
Intra-group physical conflict	Yes	Yes
Encourages overt expressions of aggressive manhood to represent toughness	Yes	Yes
Instances of death while trying to become a member	Yes	Yes
Assaults on perceived enemies	Yes	Yes
Lethal forms of retaliation	No	Yes
Endorse use of guns to settle disputes	No	Yes
Held legally accountable for selection/initiation procedures	Yes	Yes

resolved without either Set losing respect, then Sets will coexist in peace. If respect has been compromised, then there will be some level of violence, perhaps even lethal. Fraternity chapters are very similar in that they also pursue respect and seek to maintain it, so much so that they will defend their chapter's "respectability" by physical force. The major exception has been that fraternity chapters have yet to intentionally hunt and murder adversaries. Nevertheless, some chapters or individuals within chapters (from every organization--Omega Psi Phi, Kappa Alpha Psi, Phi Beta Sigma, and Alpha

Phi Alpha) have been guilty of severe attacks or assaults on individuals (fraternity members from other chapters within their own organization, members from other fraternities, un-affiliated individuals or any person(s) that are perceived to be disrespectful or threatening). Many of these episodes resulted in trips to the emergency room and even hospitalization. Black fraternities have typically demonstrated collective aggression (comparable to Hoover gangsters) as a way of "standing on manhood." Additionally, even though fraternities prohibit pledging, the pledge process still involves relatively long periods of physical hazing, (for those that want to "get down") which has been bastardized to the point of rivaling a gangster's version of being jumped in (beaten into the gang). Chapter representation, particularly for Omega Psi Phi, includes but is not limited to "going to the green," and "wrecking" (wrestling, and even fighting over trivial matters) demonstrating that (at least on the undergraduate level) there is little difference between representing a fraternity chapter and claiming a gang set. One final point of emphasis concerning Omega Psi Phi Fraternity is necessary and that is that Omega Psi Phi denounces affiliation with the canine image or any themes promoting dogmatic tendencies but the average college student with some knowledge of black Greek life will openly admit that this theme as well as others runs rampant on college campuses.

Omegas harbor the reputation for being the most aggressive and physical fraternity on campus, which is an attribute that certain types of college men gravitate towards. The appeal of Omega Psi Phi to these young men may very well be that it seems to be the institutionalized version of a street gang.

Perhaps this comparison suggests to some that black fraternities should be banned from college campuses. If you accept that, then you should also support the elimination of all major, money making, male athletic programs that recruit black men from urban areas because such activities also include some gang affiliated individuals (examine recruiting areas for the top 25 major football programs and you will find a common theme of athletes from urban areas that are most likely socially disorganized and probably ganglands). The NCAA informally recognized this problem and that is certainly one reason for changes in individual celebrations (actions that draw attention to self and take away from the team concept), a uniform dress code (that prohibited wearing bandanas, or towels with messages) and even "spatting" (taping shoes with athletic tape and writing messages on the shoe). Additionally, one would have to endorse a prohibition on sports related male group affiliations and gatherings because men in such circumstances tend to act on un-written codes of ethics requiring them to defend their honor, respectability or worth. Young men in particular (regardless of race or ethnic background) who become similarly affiliated with some group will carry out actions to promote group

loyalty, cohesiveness, and respectability. For example, white fraternities often have physical confrontations with other white fraternities and even black
groups of men at fraternity parties or in public, over perceived disrespect.
Professional sports teams (i.e. hockey, baseball, football, and basketball)
have a history of team brawls stemming from team members attempting to
stand up for other team-mates, regardless of the situation. With the exception of children's sports, every level of sport has routinely witnessed inter
and intra racial physical confrontations before, during and/or after games,
which promotes the concept of team loyalty. Sports' fans (amateur, college or
professional) will turn on one another if there is perceived disrespect. Often
times disrespect can be as trivial as showing up and supporting a team in the
opposing/enemy territory (the stadium, field-house, coliseum, etc.).

America's conventional educational institutions don't exist in a vacuum,
so when they admit students, they are accepting those students' academic
potential as well as their social and situational circumstances. Universities
provide an environment for academic excellence and healthy social relationships but they can't realistically expect a student's social background not to
continue to have some affect. After all, individuals have been socialized by
their respective environments for approximately seventeen or eighteen years
prior to college.

Additionally, contact with previous environments persists even while
students are attempting to complete a four year degree. It logically follows
that while young men seek to improve their respective life chances through
education, they remain in many ways products of their environments who
never really fully denounce their childhood associations. Young men growing
up in gang hoods across America experience varying degrees of affiliation
with gangs and some of these young men have survived their environments
and gone on to pursue college degrees (Cureton and Bellamy 2007; Cureton,
2003). Most of these former gang members who make it to college have been
recruited as athletes. It is no secret that the nation's best and worst college
football and basketball teams have had or currently have gang affiliated members on their rosters. It appears the strong arm of the gang reaches areas that
conventional society is either unaware of, or chooses to ignore so long as the
recruits conduct themselves appropriately.

Regardless of some appearances of similarities between conventional men
and ghetto males (relative to group loyalty), Americans seemingly have a
distinct fear of black gangsters because of the aura of dread black men seem
to possess (Wilson, 2009; Williams 2004; Wilson 2002; Markowitz, 2000;
Markowitz and Brown, 2000; McCall, 1994; Shakur, 1993; Anderson, 1999).
The black gangster mentality is demonized because it appears to operate
independent of rationality and; therefore, is hard to deter, socially control or

regulate. For the most part mainstream Americans, including a significant number of blacks fail to or don't care to recognize that black gangsterism is nothing more than masculinity pushed to the extreme. These young urban men are just like sports' fans (who have experienced team loss) turn on visiting fans (the perceived enemy). Only they feel as if their team is losing and continues to lose to the team called "opportunity" in the hood (their stadium, field-house, coliseum, etc.) and they feel that there is no apparent off-season. Whereas the average fan, college student, or athlete has the luxury of retreating to something conventional when the game is over, a retreat to urban residency means confronting social, economic, and subcultural trappings and vices that lead to gangsterism.

Chapter Five

One in the Chamber

Ready-Set, Aim, Now Squeeze

At the end of the day, black gangsterism places an immediate expiration date on freedom and life as evidenced by the black prison population surplus and graveyards, respectively. Certainly, this is a critical condition that needs correction and a more underclass specific movement designed to liberate a generation of disenfranchised youth from the pitfalls of gangsterism is necessary. The civil rights movement served to liberate blacks from institutional, social and cultural segregation. Unfortunately, the down-side of the movement for civil rights (arguably the most important movement for social change in the 1960's) was that it created a permanent underclass of blacks who had been abandoned by virtue of black flight. Indeed, the civil rights movement removed economic, opportunity, social, and cultural barriers and thus, integration was achieved, but at what cost? The best and brightest blacks assimilated and never looked to uplift those who were not prepared to take advantage of new (life enhancing) opportunities. As a result post civil rights permanent underclass blacks have to contend with the social fact that they are residents of an environment that will only improve with community specific personal accountability. A sincere attempt at another, liberation is the only way that young black males will be rescued from nihilism, intra-community victimization, lethal predation and imprisonment. There are so many examples of movements that have made significant social fingerprints (Moorish Science Temple, Garveyism, Black Nationalism, Civil Rights Movement, and Black Power), yet these movements failed the test of longevity and/or employed a blueprint that simply did not have generational consistency. Even though these various social movements eventually collapsed due to government pressure, the essential messages (i.e. submission to the existence of a higher spiritual energy, affirmations of black beauty/free from negative stereotyping and disciplined behavior) have the potential to transcend time (Hilliard and Zimmerman, 2006; Magida, 1996; Ture and Hamilton, 1992).

According to Cornel West

> the viability of successful democracies and/or groups attempting to improve their life chances is contingent upon intra-racial and class unity. . . . The precious notion of ordinary people living lives of decency and dignity-owing to their participation in the basic decision making in those fundamental institutions that affect their life chances-is difficult to sustain over space and time. And every historic effort to forge a democratic project has been undermined by two fundamental realities: poverty and paranoia. The persistence of poverty generates levels of despair that deepen social conflict, the escalation of paranoia produces levels of distrust that reinforce cultural division (West, 2001:155).

Revolutionary action is needed now! It will take a revolution to eradicate the nefarious conditions of the ghetto, improve structural and social living conditions, counter the rebellious nature of gangs, and disengage youth from sources that perpetuate nihilism. What can be done to help black males grasp the importance of life? An Afro-centric based coalition of federal, state, and local black leaders along with residents of urban communities should come together with one purpose in mind, the reclamation of black children. The best approach is to reverse black flight and adopt black nationalistic and black power principles. Specifically, the criminogenic nature of gangsterism has prevailed because the urban community has suffered physical and social decline. Therefore, it logically follows that a solid revolutionary effort should guarantee that every available economic, social, cultural and spiritual resource flows directly into gangland communities and remains until residents have a satisfactory standard of living. Immediate opportunities (i.e. on the job training with pay, educational/paid internships, social programs to develop artistic talents, semi-pro sports programs, infra-structure community jobs, and community/business cooperatives relative to food, clothing, and shelter) would significantly improve living conditions, decrease the need to actively participate in the underground drug economy and alternatively, reposition the gang as a leisure and perhaps secondary social network. This is where a coalition of black leaders (inclusive of upper and middle class blacks, entertainers, athletes, entrepreneurs, business executives, etc.) enters the equation by offering their talents, ideas, education, and resources to the black community. In other words, thoroughly integrated blacks, have the finances, resources, and political influence to offer enough urban aid to rebuild black communities and improve schools in the same manner that America continues to offer aid to foreign countries and assist them in their nation building efforts (Wilson, 2009; West, 2001).

Addressing the structural, economic, resource and educational needs of marginalized communities is but one part of the revolutionary equation. The success of a revolutionary reclamation project is also contingent upon functional family dynamics and positive parent/child relationships. The self-esteem of young boys (without fathers) would increase tremendously if fathers would simply reach out and try to establish a relationship with their sons. In far too many cases father/son relationships are so strained that it would seem that such a relationship is beyond repair. However, there is power in redemption, and a sincere apology by failed fathers may be all that is necessary to remove some of the anger that sons feel towards adult men and ultimately boys who are similarly circumstanced. If a son (upon) hearing an apology is willing to forgive that could be critical in the process of learning how to forgive others for their transgressions. Asking for and a willingness to forgive the transgressions of one's enemies for their war-time behaviors is an important step towards liberating black youth from a fatalistic subculture.

Another key family process component is for single mothers (who have lost their male partners due to gang wars, prison and/or abandonment) to try to avoid emasculating these men because actions and/or words intended to degrade the father ends up degrading the son.

If fathers and mothers can remove the "shame" that young boys feel then perhaps this would temper boys' boiling point, and trigger awareness of the humanity (struggles and suffering associated with poverty) of long time enemies; which could spare lives (Cureton, 2008; Williams, 2004).

Sanyika Shakur (Monster) suggests that "when gang members stop their wars and find that there is no longer a need for their sets to exist, banging will cease. But until then, all attempts by law enforcement to seriously curtail its forward motion will be in vain" (Shakur, 1993:79). Triple and Double Original Gangsters (first and second generation) from every gang set should collect all firearms from younger generations of bangers and return to settling issues using healthy alternatives (i.e. competitive sports—boxing, wrestling, football, etc). A significant action indicating forgiveness is for gangsters to uphold peace treaties. Peace treaties fail for the simple fact that peace is contingent upon the elimination of stresses, strains, and social discomforts. If these social issues can be tempered by structural, economic, social and cultural improvements in the environment (black leadership's contribution) and mediated by gangster protocols for peace then peace treaties would become more than just temporary reprieves from violence (Williams, 2004; Shakur, 1993). A non-violent gangster subculture might be impossible; however, a less lethal gangster subculture is certainly possible. The blueprint for a more civil society amongst gangsters in a gangland was constructed by Stanley "Tookie" Williams' Perpetual Peace Accord (details a peace proclamation, violation of proclamation clause, peacekeepers and monitoring committee, peacekeeper's oath, buffer zones, gang membership renunciation, and community peace accord) (Williams, 2004:364-379). Up to this point the reclamation revolution represents efforts of black people; however, once the reclamation revolution and youth liberation movement has experienced some measures of success (a steady decrease in homicide, person to person and property crimes and a decline in nuisance calls to police departments) the federal government should be approached for more financial assistance with neighborhood development (through economic, environmental, structural, housing, and employment resources). The government bares the responsibility to help disenfranchised blacks better their lives, especially when there is evidence that they are attempting to become fully engaged functional citizens.

IF ANY MAN BE REDEEMED LET HIM PROCLAIM IT

He was no angel. He was a mortal black male that was exposed to the ghetto. Crips became his response to the emasculating social facts associated with poverty. His state sponsored death was carried out on December 13, 2005. He was pronounced dead by lethal injection at 12:35am pacific time. He was a "trophy kill" a blow against black gangsterism in the gang capital of America (Becnel, 2004:348; in Williams, 2004 *Blue Rage Black Redemption*).

There is no escaping the fact that he co-founded and co-authored the most dangerous subculture that urban confined black males would routinely invest in. Crips will come and go and this is the fate of every gang member and gang that currently exists; however, the regeneration of gangsterism will remain so long as nihilism persists.

Supporters for his execution suggested that redemption was not possible in this case because there was no evidence of personal accountability. In fact, Arnold Schwarzenegger, Governor of the State of California denied clemency based on the facts of the case but also because there was no evidence of remorse. Stanley "Tookie" Williams maintained that he was innocent of the capital crimes he was convicted of, "please allow me to clarify. I will never apologize for capital crimes that I did not commit not even to save my life. And I did not commit the crimes for which I was sentenced to be executed by the State of California" (Williams, 2004:xix). Stanley "Tookie" Williams suggests that redemption is the result of soul searching and embracing themes that contradicts victimization, ignorance and support for predatory subcultures. For Mr. Williams, redemption represented a personal journey that eclipsed death by way of a resurrection. Certainly, Mr. Williams was able to transcend institutional walls and resurrect himself by speaking out against gangsterism. There is most definitely a measureable account of homicides that are gang related but there is no such measurement for the number of lives that were saved because of Stanley "Tookie" Williams. It is beyond the scope of this book to debate whether Mr. Williams' execution represented justice. Was he executed because of the capital murders he was convicted of and held legally responsible, for 24 years? Did he receive a fair trial from a jury of his peers or was he executed because he represented kingship of all things considered Crip?

Is Williams' redemption complete and sincere, or is it just a hollow promise? Stanley Williams insists he is innocent and that he will not and should not apologize or otherwise atone for the murders of the four victims in this case. Without an apology and atonement for these senseless and brutal killings there can be no redemption. In this case, the one thing that would be the clearest remorse and full redemption is the one thing Williams will not do. Clemency decisions are always difficult, and this one is no exception. After reviewing and weighing the showing Williams has made in support of his clemency request, there is nothing that compels me to nullify the jury's decision of guilt and sentence and the many court decisions during the last 24 years upholding the jury's decision with a grant of clemency. Therefore, based on the totality of circumstances in this case, Williams' request for clemency is denied (Governor Arnold Schwarzenegger, December 12, 2005).

My conviction is that redemption is achievable through God's grace and His promise of salvation. Spiritual redemption implies that the soul is at peace with God and that the soul has become liberated from the damnation of past sins. None of us can know if this was the case for Stanley "Tookie" Williams. It is a possibility that he was redeemed in ways we are not in a position to understand. *"The war within me is over, I have battled my demons and I was triumphant"* (Stanley "Tookie" Williams).

WD 40 AND KETCHUP

The nature of black gangsterism in South Central communities has continued to become so aggressive and fatalistic that researchers simply don't care to directly observe its contextual realities and behavioral outcomes. The result is that a great deal of research on black street gangs is the of result research conducted at a relative distance from the social origins of the phenomenon. The problem with this is that instead of revisiting neighborhoods to examine the complexities of coping with structural isolation, black flight, poverty, resource strain, material deprivation, exposure to deviant, criminal and violent subcultural values, underground drug and gun economy opportunities, gangster colonization and politicalization in contemporary America, dated research (1950's through 1970's) serve as a standard for how modern day black gangs operate (Cureton, 2008). The standard theme for black gangsterism is that it seems chaotic (defies the routine activities of other comparable minority deviant, violent, and criminal sub-cultural gangs), and seems genocidal (given its seemingly consistent indulgence in lethal predation). A fundamental tenet of my research on Hoover, a South Central neighborhood gang was that the field approach would reveal some authentic truisms concerning residency in one neighborhood in a gangland. Arguably, fresh information (post 1990 and on into the 21st century) on Crips and Bloods from the South Central, Los Angeles area is vital to our understanding of black male gangs because these gangs appear to represent a blueprint for gang expansion from the west to the east, in areas that don't already have traditional street gangs (who by the way exist because of similar conditions related to urban residency in socially disorganized communities). In January of 2008, *Hoover Crips: When Cripin' Becomes a Way of Life* was published. The content of the book was the result of 24 days/170 hours of field observation, interviews, and interaction. In May of 1999 I spent fourteen days and in August of 2000 I spent another ten days in South Central, observing Hoover's neighborhood and gangster culture. I observed 87 gang bangers and 10 non-gang adult residents. However, I only interviewed 12 Original Gangsters and video recorded 8, which was a decision rooted in street protocol (original gangsters must have the first opportunity), environmental social conditions (gangs wars were ongoing) and two significant social artifacts (first original gangsters had served time for their crimes and could disclose more and second these original gangsters represented the pulse of Hoover). Dr. Malcolm Klein, (a highly respected research scholar on gangs) wrote a review of my book that appeared in *Contemporary Sociology: A Journal of Reviews* (November 2008, 37[6]:587-589).

I am an admirer of Malcolm Klein's work but I was trained by Charles Tittle and Jim Short, therefore, it is in the academic spirit of these two that I respectfully respond to Klein's criticisms. Sociology should endeavor to produce meaningful appraisals, explanations, and social facts that lead to authentic understanding about an organization (Becker and Horowitz, 1972; Metzger, 1971). Additionally, "Black sociology is based on the premise that black and white people have never shared, to any great degree, the same physical environment or social experiences. The result is a different behavior pattern, a configuration that should be analyzed from the view of the oppressed-not the oppressor. Such an analysis is black sociology" (Staples, 1973: 168). The Hoover Crips and Seeds of Discontent books represent exercises in Sociology and Black Sociology simultaneously. Both books examine how gangsterism (a responsive subcultural phenomenon) became an institution within the context of structural, economic, social, and cultural deprivation. Although the Hoover book focused on one gang in South Central, Los Angeles and the Seeds of Discontent book focuses on black gangsterism as a product of race legacy in America, the evidence in both books point towards gangsterism as a product of a liberation effort (attempts to transcend marginalization, disenfranchisement, poverty, isolation, and meaninglessness). Specifically, the Emergent Gangsterism Perspective gives consideration to the probable effects of racial legacy on the black community and black experience. The Emergent Gangsterism Perspective contends that blacks have a unique history of generational humanistic deprivation that has contributed to community conversion (community stratification and a permanent underclass, segregation and isolation) and community declination, the rise of social activism and the failures of activist groups to directly address the conditions of the ghetto from which criminogenic black street gangs emerged.

The field, interview and observation methods used to gather information about the Hoover gang did permit me to offer quality information concerning the nuances (the manner in which masculinity is negotiated in a gangland, how gangsters associate and interact with one another, their customs, rituals, symbols, identification, socialization, and generational changes) of Hoovers' gangster lifestyle in one South Central neighborhood. Hoover's traditional way was that the gang was a vehicle for expression. Hoovers were about establishing a respectable identity and providing an avenue for young boys to release their aggressive energy and offering a subcultural specific viable opportunity to become ghetto superstars. Malcolm Klein suggests that the Hoover book itself (though thin) is highly valuable in the sense that it opens the door to understanding how males respond to community transition. Hence, it appears that Klein has no concerns with whether the Hoover book makes a sociological contribution rather Klein seems most concerned with the lack of ethnographic expertise, researcher divestment from the community and objectivity, measurement representation and information reliability.

Klein argues that perhaps interviewing a small number of gang veterans (older gangsters who should have matriculated out of the gang) is only good for retrospective information and does very little towards offering a contemporary vision of what gangsterism is like for young males residing on Hoover. I clearly admitted that the focus on Original gangsters served the purpose of adding a measure of full disclosure given those interviewed had served time for their crimes and could therefore be truthful more than boastful. Additionally, the gangsters that I talked to were still involved in the gang (they had not matriculated out of the gang) and in fact were higher ranking members in the gang. What this means is that the Original gangsters I interviewed were directly linked to younger generation of bangers. The social fact about modern day gangsterism is that gang members stay in the gang longer (and this is due in part to an inability to successfully integrate and/or become functional citizens) and gangsters' street monikers that begin with little, baby, and infant, identifies what generation of bangers you are dealing with. Triple Original Gangsters have usually retired from the trivial matters of gangsterism but still invest in how their gang set is represented and they are also essential in peace treaties. Double Original and Original gangsters represent second and third generation gangsters who continue to be directly involved in the day to day operations of the street gang. Double and Original Gangsters provide a measure of consistency for little, baby, and infant gangsters who are fourth, fifth and sixth generation bangers, respectively. Therefore, when I interviewed Duck, Mad Dog, Big Frog, Man, Chim, Twin and Sniper, I was dealing with Double and Original gangsters who represented the pulse of Hoover. Moreover, whatever information I ascertained from younger gangbangers was integrated in the book without specifics to attaching names because these young bangers represented a group of criminals that may not have necessarily been held legally accountable for their actions.

Klein contends that there were issues of validity as the gangster's stories could not be corroborated and the fact that interviews were done in public negatively, impacted the information that gangsters disclosed. Certainly, any experienced field researcher would understand how peer pressure could negatively impact interview information and I did acknowledge this as a social artifact or caveat in my research, "it could possibly be the case that their presence contributed to masculine boasting.... I learned that Hoover gangsters are a bit more critical of what their peers say than one would imagine. Thus, their presence probably limited the amount of lying because gangsters' confessed realities become their spoken word" (Cureton, 2008:61). I have been academically disciplined enough not to take information at face value and I do recognize that revelations or story telling (retrospect or otherwise) can be tainted with social artifacts (interview effects, location, time, situation and circumstance). The civility of Hoover was balanced by the ugly realities of Hoover and the fact that these were equally disclosed was enough for me to move forward with presenting Hoover gangsterism in the manner that it was presented to me. Moreover, I think that Malcolm Klein grossly underestimated the kind of research instrument I represent.

I am not a newcomer to the contextual realities of urban poverty. My life course does equip me with enough social currency to effectively observe those things that were being practiced in plain sight.

Malcolm Klein continues to suggest that communities don't easily open up to researchers in 24 days and I can respect this criticism as relatively true. However, I did not engage in what Du Bois would call "car window sociology" (Du Bois, 1953:116). The work put into Hoover may not measure up to

Klein's expectations but it was far more than leisure hours or observations void of contact with the neighborhoods and the people. It seems to me that Klein (in typical fashion to most men who are not black) fails to understand and grasp the potential power of universal black brotherhood. There is no denying who I gravitate towards and who gravitates towards me. I honor and respect that and completely embrace it because before anything and above everything I am a black researcher, the gangsters I interviewed are black, together we are black and I can comfortably call them my race brothers. And as for the community, the parents of gangsters and even those who have been victimized by the awful realities of gangs, disclosed realities to me that I bet others would have a hard time getting. In short, Hoover embraced me and still does (gangsters and residents) to the point where I still have "bedding, a meal, fellowship and conversation." I continue to be well taken care of by a number of black men who just so happen to be members of various gangs in South Central.

Klein also criticizes the Hoover book for being a-historical to the degree that gangsters seemed to not recognize their historical roots. This could have been true of the gangsters as they did routinely suggest that Cripin' originated in the latter part of the 1960's and early 1970's. Where Klein implies that I am not cognizant of the history of gangsterism, I would suggest that he revisit the argument set forth in the Emergent Gangsterism Perspective. I am aware that modern day gangsterism is the result of an inheritance. Indeed gangsterism has everything to do with inheritance, but don't stop there, Malcolm. Gangsterism is the result of inheriting not just decades of turf traditions but centuries of inequitable, discretionary, discriminatory, and racist Americanism. It is true that modern day gangs have roots in Slausons, Businessmen, Gladiators, Pirus, Bounty Hunters and other traditional gangs. Let's faithfully carry out the argument set forth in the Hoover book. Gangs were a product of social activism that was derailed by the strong arm tactics of the government during the gangster colonization (1966-1989) stage of community evolution. Nevertheless, I can see what Klein was trying to get at so this book, *Seeds of Discontent* further elaborates on how gangsterism is the product of a negative race legacy that prompted a spirit of rebellion.

Finally, Klein criticized my full disclosure of my spirituality. He argues that it is unusual and could be viewed as an intrusion by readers. I somewhat agree; however, in the face of circumstances (my life course triumphs leading up to my research on Hoovers who at the time were engaged in gang wars with death and the misery of burying dead young adults and children) it is hard to remain a detached social scientist and not profess the Spiritual Energy that guides me. If there be anyone who think this position is not appropriate, I offer this was the same position that Du Bois subscribed too when he was faced with investigating the deteriorating social life circumstances of the Negro.

We seldom study the condition of the Negro today honestly and carefully. It is so much easier to assume that we know it all. Or perhaps, having already reached conclusions in our own minds, we are loth to have them disturbed by facts. And yet how little we really know of these millions, of their daily lives and longings, of their homely joys, and sorrows, of their real shortcomings and the meaning of their crimes! All this we can learn by intimate contact with the masses, and not by wholesale arguments covering millions separate in time and space and differing widely in training culture (Du Bois, 1953:105).

It could be that Malcolm Klein's academic tire treads are a little worn (that can happen with academic longevity). It could also be the case that Malcolm Klein is a little bit rusty when it comes to walking Hoover turf; even though the University of Southern California rests on the better end of Hoover! If Malcolm Klein is suggesting that the Hoover product suffered because of my inexperience in the field, I have to say that perhaps his "expertise" is outdated, racially stagnant and tired. Therefore, the WD 40 is for the rust, and the ketchup is street terminology for "you need to catch-up." One final note, Malcolm I am not mad at you, even though you thought I would be but you had to know I would not let your review ride. That's just not, well for lack of a better word, gangster.

AFTER THOUGHTS

If the black community fails to capitalize on universal brotherhood by moving forward with a revolution to reclaim and liberate disenfranchised youth, then the black community is guilty of neglect, abandonment and murder. This book was inspired by all of the gangsters I have had the pleasure of meeting and breaking bread with since the Hoover book was published in 2008. I have heard you all loud and clear and recognize the need to continue the war against a-historical presentations of black gangsterism. I understand that there are many ways to put in work and putting in work is not limited to the streets of ganglands in most urban areas across the country. The social landscape of mis-information is bountiful and there is a desperate need to counter ignorance with knowledge. Except for the potential of a new liberation, the trappings of gangsterism will prevail.

What is it going to take for brothers to keep it pushing as William Fields would say. When will that black prince come along with the sense to have read the end of Stan "Tookie" Williams' *Blue Rage Black Redemption*? The blueprint for overcoming the most devastating subculture to affect young black males residing in ganglands has already been offered. Who will be the person or persons to pick up that torch?

References

Agnew, Robert (2006). *Pressured into Crime: An Overview of General Strain Theory.* California: Roxbury Publishing Group.

Agnew, Robert (2005). *Why Do Criminals Offend?: A General Theory of Crime and Delinquency.* California: Roxbury Publishing Company.

Alonso, Alejandro (1999). *Territoriality Among African-American Street Gangs in Los Angeles.* Unpublished Master's Thesis. University of Southern California.

Anderson, Elijah (1999). *Code of the Street.* New York: W.W. Norton and Company.

Anderson, Elijah (1990). *StreetWise.* Chicago: The University of Chicago Press.

Asbury, Herbert (1928). *The Gangs of New York.* New York: Alfred Knopf.

Ashmore, Harry (1997). *Civil Rights and Wrongs: A Memoir of Race and Politics 1944–1996.* South Carolina: University of South Carolina Press.

Becker, Howard and Horowitz, Irving (1972) Radical Politics and Sociological Research: Observations on Methodology and Ideology. *American Journal of Sociology* 78(1)48–66.

Benedict, Ruth (1934). *Patterns of Culture.* New York: First Mariner Books.

Bennett, Lerone (1961). *Before the Mayflower: A History of Black America.* New York: Penguin Press.

Bing, Leon (1991). *Do or Die.* New York: HarperCollins.

Blauner, Robert (1969). Internal Colonialism and Ghetto Revolt. *Social Problems.* 16(4)393–408.

Brown, Waln (1999). Black Female Gangs in Philadelphia in Meda Chesney-Lind and John Hagedorn's (eds.) *Female Gangs in America.* Chicago: Lakeview Press.

Byman, Daniel (2008). *The Five Front War: The Better Way to Fight Global Jihad.* New Jersey: John Wiley and Sons Inc.

Clark, Kenneth (1966). The Civil Rights Movement: Momentum and Organization, *Journal of the American Academy of Arts and Sciences.* 95(1)241–264.

Cleaver, Eldridge (1968). *Soul on Ice.* New York: Random House.

Cloward, Richard and Ohlin, Lloyd (1962). Subcultural Differentiation. In M. Wolfgang, L. Savitz and N. Johnston (Eds.) *The Sociology of Crime and Delinquency.* New York: Wiley and Sons.

Cloward, Richard and Ohlin, Lloyd (1960). *Delinquency and Opportunity: A Theory of Delinquent Gangs.* New York: Free Press.

Cohen, Albert (1955). *Delinquent Boys: The Culture of the Gang.* New York: Free Press.

Cone, James (2003). *Martin, Malcolm and America: A Dream or a Nightmare.* New York: Orbis Books.

Corbiscello, G. V. (2004). A Nation of Gods: The Five Percent Nation of Islam. In G. Knox and C. Robinson (Eds.), *Gang Profiles: An Anthology.* Illinois: New Chicago Press.

Cross, William. (1973). The Negro-to-Black Conversion Experience. In J. Ladner (Ed.) *The Death of White Sociology.* New York: Vintage Books.

Cureton, Steven (2009). Something Wicked This Way Comes: A Historical Account of Black Gangsterism Offers Wisdom and Warning for African-American Leadership. *Journal of Black Studies,* 40(2):347–361.

Cureton, Steven (2008). *Hoover Crips: When Cripin' Becomes a Way of Life.* Lanham, MD: University Press of America.

Cureton, Steven (2007). Gangster 'Blood' over College Aspirations: The Implications of Gang Membership for One Black Male College Student. *Journal of Gang Research* 14(2):31–49.

Cureton, Steven (2003). Race Specific College Student Experiences on a Predominantly White Campus. *Journal of Black Studies,* 33(3):295–311.

Cureton, Steven (2002a). An Assessment of Wilson and Frazier's Perspective on Race and Racial Life Chances, *African American Research Perspectives,* 8(1)47–54.

Cureton, Steven (2002b). Introducing Hoover: I'll Ride for you Gangsta in Huff's (ed.) *Gangs in America,* 3rd Edition. Thousand Oaks: Sage.

Dawley, David (1992). *A Nation of Lords.* Illinois: Waveland Press Inc.

Dreer, Herman (1940). *The History of the Omega Psi Phi Fraternity: A Brotherhood of Negro College Men, 1911–1939.* U.S. America; Published by Omega Psi Phi Fraternity.

Dyson, Michael (1996). *Race Rules: Navigating the Color Line.* New York: Vintage Books.

Du Bois, W.E. Burghardt (1953). *Souls of Black Folk: Essays and Sketches.* Connecticut: Fawcett Publications.

Fields, William (2008). *House of Failure.* California: Cupidity Press.

Fishman, Laura (1999). Black Female Gang Behavior: An Historical and Ethnographic Perspective in Meda Chesney-Lind and John Hagedorn's (eds.) *Female Gangs in America.* Chicago: Lakeview Press. Pp 64–84.

Fishman, Laura (1995). The Vice Queens: An Ethnographic Study of Black Female Gang Behavior in Malcolm Klein, Cheryl Maxson and Jody Miller's (eds.) *The Modern Gang Reader.* California: Roxbury Publishing Company.

Franklin, Raymond (1966). The Political Economy of Black Power, *Social Problems,* (16)286–301.

Frazier, Franklin E. (1968). *Race Relations*. Chicago: The University of Chicago Press.

Frazier, Franklin E. (1957). *Black Bourgeoisie*. New York: Collier Macmillan Publishers.

Foner, Philip (1970). *The Black Panthers Speak*. New York: DA Capo Press.

Gabbidon, Shaun and Helen, Taylor Greene (2009). *Race and Crime* (2nd Edition). California: Sage Publications.

Garrow, David (1953). *The FBI and Martin Luther King, Jr.* New York: Penguin Books.

Geschwender, James (1971). *The Black Revolt: The Civil Rights Movement, Ghetto Uprisings, and Separatism*. New York: Prentice Hall.

Geschwender, James and Singer Benjamin (1971). The Detroit Insurrection: Grievance and Facilitating Conditions in Geschwender (ed.) *The Black Revolt: The Civil Rights Movement, Ghetto Uprisings and Separatism*. New Jersey: Prentice Hall.

Gill, Robert (1963). *The Omega Psi Phi Fraternity and the Men Who Made Its History: A Concise History, 1911–1961*. U.S. America: Published by Omega Psi Phi Fraternity.

Golding, William (1954). *Lord of the Flies*. New York: Perigree.

Gottfredson, Michael and Hirschi, Travis (1990). *A General Theory of Crime*. California: Stanford University Press.

Hagedorn, John (1988). *People and Folks: Gangs, Crime, and The Underclass in Rustbelt City*. Chicago: Lakeview Press.

Haley, Alex (1964). *The Autobiography of Malcolm X*. New York: Ballantine Books.

Hilliard, David and Zimmerman, Keith and Zimmerman, Kent (2006). *Huey: Spirit of the Panther*. New York: Thunder's Mouth Press.

Hilliard, David, and Weise, Donald (2002). *The Huey P. Newton Reader*. New York: Seven Stories Press.

Hutchinson, Earl (1998). *The Crisis in Black and Black*. California: Middle Passage Press.

Jackson, George (1994). *Soledad Brother: The Prison Letters of George Jackson*. Chicago: Lawrence Hill Books.

Jackson, Ronald (2006**).** *Scripting the black masculine body: Identity Discourse and Racial Politics in Popular Media*. Albany: State University of New York Press.

Katz, Jack (1988). *Seductions of Crime: Moral and Sensual Attractions In Doing Evil*. New York: Basic Books.

Keegan, Frank (1971). *BlackTown U.S.A.* Boston: Little, Brown, and Company.

Killian, Lewis (1972) The Significance of Extremism in the Black Revolution. *Social Problems*. 20(1)41–49.

Killian, Lewis and Smith Charles (1960) Negro Protest Leaders in a Southern Community, *Social Forces* 38:253–257.

Knox, George (2009). *An Introduction to Gangs*. 6th Edition. Illinois: New Chicago School Press.

Knox, George. (2004a). Gang Profile: Black P. Stone Nation. In G. Knox and C. Robinson (Eds.), *Gang Profiles: An Anthology*, Illinois: New Chicago Press.

Knox, George. (2004b). Gang Profile: The Black Disciples. In G. Knox and C. Robinson (Eds.), *Gang Profiles: An Anthology*, Illinois: New Chicago Press.

Knox, G. (2004c). A Comparison of Two Gangs: The Gangster Disciples and the Vice Lords. In G. Knox and C. Robinson (Eds.), *Gang Profiles: An Anthology,* Illinois: New Chicago Press.

Knox, George. (2004d). The Melanics: A Gang Profile Analysis. In G. Knox and C. Robinson (Eds.), *Gang Profiles: An Anthology,* Illinois: New Chicago Press.

Knox, George and Fuller, Leslie (2004). The Gangster Disciples: A Gang Profile. In G. Knox and C. Robinson (Eds.), *Gang Profiles: An Anthology,* Illinois: New Chicago Press.

Knox, George and Papachristos, Andrew (2002). *The Vice Lords: A Gang Profile Analysis.* Illinois: New Chicago Press.

Knox, George (2000). *An Introduction to Gangs,* 5th Edition. Illinois: New Chicago School Press.

Ladner, Joyce (1967). What "Black Power" Means to Negroes in Mississippi. *TRANS-action Magazine,* pp.7–15.

Lightfoot, Claude (1968*). Ghetto Rebellion to Black Liberation.* New York: International Publishers.

Leet, Duane and Rush, George and Smith, Anthony. (1997). *Gangs Graffiti and Violence: A Realistic Guide to the Scope and Nature of Gangs in America.* Nevada: Copperhouse Publishing Company.

Lincoln, Eric (1961). *The Black Muslims in America.* Boston: Beacon Press.

Magida, Arthur (1996). *The Prophet of Rage: A Life of Louis Farrakhan and His Nation.* New York: Basic Books.

Marable, Manning (1998). *Speaking Truth to Power: Essays on Race, Resistance, and Radicalism.* Colorado: Westview Press.

Marable, Manning (1997). *Black Liberation in Conservative America.* Boston: South End Press.

Markowitz, Michael (2000). Theoretical Explanations of the Nexus between Race and Crime in Markowitz and Jones-Brown's (eds.) *The System in Black and White: Exploring the Connections between Race, Crime, and Justice.* Connecticut: Praeger.

McCall, Nathan (1994). *Makes Me Wanna Holler: A Young Black Man in America.* New York: Random House.

McCarthy, John, and Yancey, William (1971). Uncle Tom and Mr. Charlie: Metaphysical Pathos in the Study of Racism and Personal Disorganization. *American Journal of Sociology,* 76(4)648–672.

McCorkle, Richard, and Miethe, Terance (2002). *Panic: The Social Construction of the Street Gang Problem.* New Jersey: Prentice Hall.

Meier, August and Rudwick, Elliott (1966). *From Plantation to Ghetto.* New York: Hill and Wang.

Merton, Thomas (1948). *The Seven Storey Mountain: An Autobiography of Faith.* Florida: Harcourt Inc.

Metzger, Paul (1971). American Sociology and Black Assimilation: Conflicting Perspectives. *American Journal of Sociology.* 76(4)627–647.

Miller, Walter (1975). *Violence by Youth Gangs and Youth Groups: As A Crime Problem In Major American Cities.* Washington D.C. U.S. Government Printing Office.

Miller, Walter (1958). Lower Class Culture as Generating Milieu of Gang Delinquency. *Journal of Social Issues,* 14:5–19.

Markowitz, Michael and Jones-Brown, Delores (eds.)(2000). *The System in Black and White: Exploring the Connections between Race, Crime, and Justice.* Connecticut: Praeger.

Nisbet, Robert (1996). *The Sociological Tradition.* New York: Holt and Rinehart.

Obserschall, Anthony (1967). The Los Angeles Riot of August 1965. *Social Problems* 15:322–341.

Oliver, William (1989). Black Males and Social Problems: Prevention Through Afrocentric Socialization. *Journal of Black Studies,* 20:15–39.

Phares, Walid (2008). *The Confrontation: Winning the War Against Future Jihad.* England: Palgrave MacMillan.

Pitts, James (1974). The Study of Race Consciousness: Comments on New Directions. *American Journal of Sociology,* 80(3)665–687.

Quarantelli, E.L. and Dynes, Russell (1970) Property Norms and Looting: Their Patterns in Community Crisis. Phylon: *The Atlanta University Review of Race and Culture,* 31–168–172.

Raboteau, Albert (1978). *Slave Religion: The Invisible Institution in the Antebellum South.* New York: Oxford University Press.

Raper, Arthur (1933). *The Tragedy of Lynching.* North Carolina: The University of North Carolina Press.

Shakur, Sanyika (1993). *Monster: The Autobiography of an L.A. Gang Member.* New York: Penguin Books.

Shaw, Clifford, and McKay, Henry (1942*). Juvenile Delinquency and Urban Areas.* Chicago: University of Chicago Press.

Short, James, F. (1997). *Poverty, Ethnicity, and Violent Crime.* Colorado: Westview Press.

Skogan, Wesley (1990). *Disorder and Decline: Crime and The Spiral of Decay in American Neighborhoods.* New York: Free Press.

Simons, Ronald and Simons, Leslie Gordon and Wallace, Lora Ebert (2004). *Families Delinquency and Crime: Linking Society's Most Basic Institution to Antisocial Behavior.* California: Roxbury Publishing Company.

Sloan, Cle "Bone" (2007). *Bastards of the Party.* Home Box Office Documentary Film produced by Cle "Bone" Sloan and Antoine Fuqua.

Staples, Robert (1973). What is Black Sociology? Toward a Sociology of Black Liberation in Joyce Ladner (ed.) *The Death of White Sociology,* New York: Vintage Books.

Stewart, Eric, and Simons, Ronald (2006). Structure and Culture in African-American Adolescent Violence: A Partial Test of the "Code of the Street" Thesis. *Justice Quarterly* 23(1):1–29.

Stewart, Eric, and Schreck, Christopher, and Simons, Ronald (2006). "I Ain't Gonna Let no One Disrespect Me" Does the Code of the Street Reduce or Increase Violent Victimization among African-American Adolescents? *Journal of Research in Crime and Delinquency* 43(4):427–458.

Short, James and Strodtbeck, Fred. (1965). *Group Process and Gang Delinquency.* Chicago: University of Chicago Press.

Suttles, Gerald. (1972). *The Social Construction of Communities.* Chicago: University of Chicago Press.

Taylor, Carl (1990). *Dangerous Society.* Michigan: Michigan State University Press.

Thrasher, Frederic. (1927). *The Gang.* Chicago: University of Chicago Press.

Tittle, Charles and Paternoster, Raymond (2000). *Social Deviance and Crime: An Organizational and Theoretical Approach.* California: Roxbury Publishing Company.

Tucker, Sterling (1968). *Beyond the Burning: Life and Death of the Ghetto.* New York: Association Press.

Ture, Kwame and Hamilton, Charles (1992). *Black Power: The Politics of Liberation.* New York: Vintage Books.

Voisin, Dexter and Guilamo-Ramos, Vincent (2008). A Commentary on Community Violence Exposure and HIV Risk Behaviors among African-American Adolescents. *African-American Research Perspectives,* 12(1):83–100.

Wanderer, Jules (1969). An Index of Riot Severity and Some Correlates, *The American Journal of Sociology* 74:500–505.

Washington, Harriet (2006). *Medical Apartheid: The Dark History of Medical Experimentation on Black Americans from Colonial Times to the Present.* New York: Harlem Moon/Broadway Books.

Washington, Booker T. (1967) *Up From Slavery.* New York: Airmont Books.

Walker, Samuel and Spohn, Cassia and Delone, Miriam (2007). *The Color of Justice: Race, Ethnicity, and Crime in America.* California: Thomson Wadsworth.

West, Cornel (2001). *Race Matters.* New York: Vintage Books.

Williams, Mary (1995). *Examining Issues Through Political Cartoons: Civil Rights.* California: GreenHaven Press.

Williams, "Tookie" Stanley (2004). *Blue Rage Black Redemption.* California: Damamli Publishing Company.

Wilson, Ebony (2002). *Breaking the Cycle: From Special Ed. To Ph.D.* Washington: Peanut Butter Publishing.

Wilson, William Julius (2009). *More Than Just Race: Being Black and Poor in the Inner City.* New York: W.W. Norton and Company.

Wilson, William Julius (1996). *When Work Disappears: The World of the New Urban Poor.* New York: Knopf.

Wilson, William, Julius (1987). *The Truly Disadvantaged: The Inner City, The Underclass, and Public Policy.* Chicago: University of Chicago Press.

Wilson, William, Julius (1978*). The Declining Significance of Race.* Chicago: The University of Chicago Press.

Wilson, James and Herrnstein Richard (1985). *Crime and Human Nature.* New York: Simon & Schuster. Woodson, Carter (1933), *The Mis-Education of the Negro.* Chicago: African-American Images.

Young, Vernetta, and Greene Taylor, 1995 Incorporating African American Perspectives Into the Curriculum. *Journal of Criminal Justice Education,* 6(1) 85–104.

CPSIA information can be obtained at www.ICGtesting.com
Printed in the USA
BVOW070842031111

274950BV00003B/3/P